सुप्रीम ईश्वर के निर्देश

INSTRUCTIONS OF THE SUPREME GOD

AF613173

श्री सुनीता माचरा शक्ति

SHREE SUNITA MACHRA SHAKTI

(B. SC. (BIOLOGY) , M. A. (ENGLISH) , GNM , MBA (HRM) , MSW , RS - CIT)

© **Shree Sunita Machra Shakti 2021**

All rights reserved

All rights reserved by author. No part of this publication may be reproduced, stored in a retrieval system or transmitted in any form or by any means, electronic, mechanical, photocopying, recording or otherwise, without the prior permission of the author.

Although every precaution has been taken to verify the accuracy of the information contained herein, the author and publisher assume no responsibility for any errors or omissions. No liability is assumed for damages that may result from the use of information contained within.

First Published in December 2021

ISBN: 978-93-5472-609-5

BLUEROSE PUBLISHERS

www.bluerosepublishers.com

info@bluerosepublishers.com

+91 8882 898 898

Cover Design:

Geetika

Typographic Design:

Namrata Saini

Distributed by: BlueRose, Amazon, Flipkart, Shopclues

PART - 1

1. WORK STYLE OF THE ALIENS

There is an another world apart from this physical world we called which the " SPIRITUAL WORLD ". Holy divine spirits are live in it. The supreme god shree ancient power jee is all their producer & director. There are various godlicy forms according to work, their vehicles, aliens & UFOs are work in her direction. They all are alive. Ten astrological planets & their vehicles are also alive. Only earth & air are alive among the five matters (earth, sky, water, fire & air) which make a live creature ' s body. The sky is a media. Air is vitality — vitality is soul & the soul is the life. These all are meritorious and having their own structure. But the third eye is necessary to see them with somebody. The devotion & doings are crucial to achieving the third eye which is given by the supreme god to someone. Mean by devotion is duly worshipping without any ritualism & doings mean is servicing to needy - helpless with charity - virtue by obedience and morality at appropriate time.

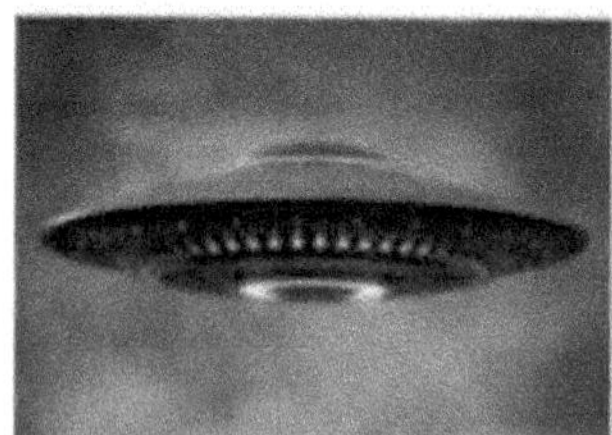

UFO ALIENS

UFOs are the divine vehicles of aliens and aliens are godlicy robots which are wandering into heaven, hell, on the earth and over all the cosmos. Aliens have not any their physical body as the god but they are labour divine souls of the kingdom which are regularly working for various godlicy forms. They are angels of the god. Aliens are carry the soul of a dead person after his / her death from someone ' s dead body on its ' complete age. Aliens visible as a black shadow to the dead person ' s soul.

Today, there are not any deity & divinity in the nature because they all are rebirthed whether they were from any caste, religion, denomination & country. Monsters have been entered in hell for unlimited time. All godlicy forms (as - shree gajaanand jee - ancient power jee - shivparvati jee - brahmasaraswati jee - laxmivishnu jee - seetaramchandra jee - hanuman jee - ten planet jee), their vehicles, aliens & UFOs are noneffective from hunger - thrust - weather and climate.

Aliens are godlicy robot which are connected by internet connection with mutually each - another, UFOs, various godlicy forms & their vehicles from equal frequently brain waves by knowing mutually same knowledge and with same to the god. Aliens are human shaped which have two upper limb, two lower limb & the brain is all over of the body because the maximum energy & brain power is included in it form. So the gradual development process of the kingdom was stopped after making the human body. All works of whole the cosmos are done by aliens in the observation of various godlicy forms. Aliens are connected with every creatures ' s brain for every moment. They see, read & write online (rather, there are not any physical record in the heaven) his / her sentiments & doings so that they can enter the creature in the heaven or the hell after it ' s death & can determine to it ' s rebirth based on it ' s doings of prebirth. The energy of aliens & UFOs are unlimited, positive & upwarding. Due to omnipresent of aliens the various forms of the god are omnipresrnt.

Aliens are machine men. Whenever i met to them all the same i watched them in combatised soldiers as - sometimes in gray khaki police uniform, sometimes in white warriors uniform, sometimes in robot form etc. One day in my dream, when i met to them then they stood in white warriors uniform with maintaining social distancing in desert ground. Then i thought in my mind that my exam was so near and i was not knowing about exam ' s matter then how i could appear in exam. Then they recognized my problem without any talking with me and they gave to me all exam related notes without any computer - printer - photocopier. Thus, their age, work power and brain power are unlimited. Robot (machine men) are made by human on inspiration of god on imitate of aliens.

2. FORETELLINGS BY NOSTRADAMUS - II

The scholar & great " CHEYREN " of ASIA will be received respect as dove winner in all the countries. Meanwhile will threaten he / she by an " ALUS " named bloody dangerous man. But in the last his / her hand will be reached till bloody alus & alus will be failured to run by sea way. Army will encircled him in the middle of two rivers. Fierce black will punished him because of his defaults. As leader of the east he / she will evacuated by air path. He / she will be zapped his / her mace bygoing upon the air, water & ice. He / she will watch the italian mountains and france.

There will be collided fierce black - white & red - yellow between those two for their own rights.

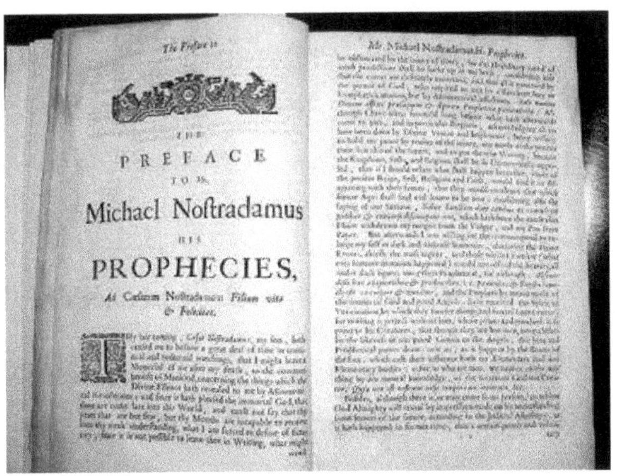
PREFACE

Michael Noſtradamus

PROPHECIES,

NOSTRADAMUS PROPHECIES.

The explanations : --

1. Here the word " CHEYREN " is used for me. My birth astrological name is starting from " CH " (CHOONIYA) & shree Nostradamus jee gave me Cheyren name.

SHREE SUNITA MACHRA SHAKTI

2. Here is mean by bloody Alus is monster " KAAL BHAIRAV " & his seven members ladies team.

3. Two men effected by alus monster are my elder brother jee & my young nefhew. They two were suffered from frenzy disease because of their brain washing by a savage occultist. They both were from out of control of family members & usually came to grief with road accident in wine intoxication. But I saved them from danger by my god worshipping & charity - virtue alive & safe. At last better from one - another, by please of three fierce black jee. Now they both are completely out of frenzy disease and are living prosperous and healthy life.

4. Here the word " sea " is mean by my so voluminous heart in which there are fulfilled all godlicy forms and their vehicles of whole cosmos. These all are staying in " PACEMAKER " which is a nervous controller of the heart. Pacemaker is situated at the middle wall of the heart between left semi part & right semi part.

5. Whereas present time is the time of biological warfare in place of weapon warfare so here " TWO RIVERS " are mean by right impure blood part and left pure blood part of my heart between which is situated the pacemaker.

6. Here the word " ARMY " is mean by various godlicy forms & their vehicles situated in my heart. They all surrounded to the monsters.

7. I have three fierce black jee as -- The " ELEPHANT JEE (devine vehicle of shree " SHANI JEE "), self shree " SHANI JEE " and shree " KING COBRA JEE ". These three discarded monsters in the hell.

8. I will go to Europe & USA by air path to achieving various prizes from there.

9. Here white colour is of bloody monster alus who was very struggled to fence his existence but he annihilated by three fierce black jee.

10. Here the word " RED - YELLOW " is mean by occultists who were snatched money and reverence of public by their brainwashing. Occultists were displayed to voodoism, magical charm, bewitchment, black magic, isolationism and terrorism in return of the money. I am sorry that an occultist adored to monster kaal bhairav with the prime minister of my country on the occation of the Earth adoration for the god shree Seetaramchandra jee levee. Then i was watching it incident on television. Since i was not disclosured at that time so i could not objection it. Then i chased monster from there silently as soon.

11. My humble appeal from all the general public that they should to transplant six godlicy form ' s idols / pictures on location of monster ' s idols / pictures without any violence - sabotage and should to start worshipping six pictures

3. SHREE BRAHMA JEE

Disclosuring of shree Brahmajee happened as form of my father shree Multanchand machra on 04 october, 1949 AD in a poor - rural - farmer family. His father was shree Tulchharam machra. My father borned at v / p - baytu bheemajee, tehsil - baytu, distt - barmer, state - rajasthan (INDIA). He was smallest in five brothers & sisters (three brothers + two sisters). His mother smt. Mirgon devi expired in his 18 months age. After that his father & two elder sisters nourished, blowed up & taught him. He was a single educated person in his family. My grand father worked at farms and alongwith he worked to inching on wood & stones.

SHREE MULTAN CHAND MACHRA

First elder. brother of my father was expired in his own 16 yrs age. My father ' s marriage held in his 9 years immature age with smt. Bhooree devee but their gauna (real marriage) held on his 17 years age when he was studying in BSTC training. He posted on 3 rd grade teacher post on his 18 yrs age. My two aunts had gone to their father in law ' s family until. My elder brother shree Deepak kumar machra borned at 26 december, 1968 when my father was 19 yrs old. After that in few days my grand father & my elder father was expired in time gap of one month of " cholera " disease. Then responsibility of my elder mother & her two daughters (smt. Champa machra & smt. Damyanti machra), came & beliefed on my parents.

MY PARENTS

My grandfather & elder father were loanee of somebodies so my father discounted their loans & it ' s interests by his salary of 100 /- rupees. My father gave return mortgaged ornaments of my elder mother to her. Many times faced to famine. With increasing of his salary, my father helped his sister ' s families & some other poor families also. My elder sister smt. Kamla machra borned at 17 february 1971 & i was borned at 03 october, 1974 (thursday) AD.

We four, brother & sisters

I am 3 rd child of four. My younger sister Bhagwati machra borned at 22 april, 1977. Usually my father wrote an annual diaries in every year. He wrote one diary on his all life in which aur birth incidents was comedy incidents and someone ' s death in aur family was tragedy incident. My mother was house wife & my father taught her till class 8 th. My mother did agreeculture & animal husbandry alongwith home works. We all brothers & sisters did help her in every work. My father achieved higher and further education alongwith his govt service. He got medical science study & treated poor people with his govt job at an appropriate cost. My mother helped to my father by saling her minimum available ornaments for his further study & training. Rather, my father made

& gave return all types ornaments to my mother. My father was promoted again and again in his service because of his higher educational qualifications from a 3 rd grade teacher to lecturer. In the last he was retired from the post of education extension officer at 31 october, 2009. He have total 7 educational degrees, diplomas & certificates as : - BSTC, BA., B.ED., MA, M.ED., VAIDYA VISHAARAD & AYURVEDA RATNA.

My father was very great and high stratified thoughtfull person who worked at the principle of " THE WHOLE WORLD IS A FAMILY " & lived with commingling to all. He nourished & taught to we all children since 50 yrs ago from today. People did not taught their children at that time & absolutely not taught to their daughters. He nourished, taught and erected marry of my elder father ' s daughters. Today we all six brothers & sisters are doing govt jobs.

But he did not disclosured in his life that he was a pure heavenly spirit of god shree Brahma jee because he did not do any devotion in his all life for a minute. In 2012 when he was very suffered from cancer disease then i said to him to invoke the Gayatri jee chant and shree Hanuman jee chalisa but he refused me clearly for it.

Whereas, god shree Brahma jee is father of all the earthlings so shree Brahma jee himself borned on the earth to produce the supreme god shree ancient power jee. You, all earthlings are scattered into various castes, religions, denominations & nations --- you all worshipped the various forms of the god on various places separately who are inhabitant of a single heaven so there was established a lack of mutually comprehension & adjustment in the heaven among all the godlicy forms. It ' s damages endured to all earthlings in it way that the Brahmajee unless stayed on the world of death till 64 years yet in absence of his, aliens could not write the fate of neonate children from the heaven as properly. So today ' s many people happened with ominous characteristics as terrorism, saperalism, racism, deceit, men thumper & self thumper etc.

At now, we both father & daughter trying to reconcile wrong written & neonate ' s fate of population continuously. He well taught to me and made able. He established many innovations in the society but could not repair the evils prevailed in the kingdom because he was not the fullflash god and was not full from omnicompetent. I knew before 20 days of his death that he was the pure soul holder from heaven of shree Brahma jee. But he self did not know that he was a sacred soul. He died of cancer disease on 06 november, 2013 AD but it was only a worldly pretext. The original reason was - his hard need in the heaven to redress the accounts of earthling ' s destinies.

Although, this topic was sat down in his heart ' s corner so he usually said to me that no any earthling worships to god shree Brahma jee & did not make god Brahma jee's worship place and if someone do so then he died. Because shree Brahmajee is the father / producer of all earthlings then a son / daughter can not produce his / her father. Now, we changed this custom and started the worshipping of shree Brahmajee with his wife shree Saraswati jee. The worshipping of the god as a form of couple is completely prosperous. By it the families of earthlings become stable - persistant & blossom. Today, no any person worshipping to my father saperately as an idol / picture because we entered him into the ancient Brahma jee. Earthlings should worship to only six idols/ pictures.

4. I AM

The goddess of the knowledge shree Saraswati jee & the goddess of the wealth shree Laxmi jee are also the copies of mine. They are unborned & self styled whom i made by my yoga & maya. It means that i am three in one. Rather, all other self styled (who are unborned & of non parentile) godlicy forms are made by my yoga & maya so i am all in one.

I have safely ascendancy of all godlicy forms. I have infinitive work power & unlimited brainpower. So in the future time whenever, presence of the god will be necessary on the earth then i will be borned & will be disclosured on it. We will not forwarded to god shree Brahma jee before me. I will borned in any general family anywhere & at anytime.

MY SMALLEST UNIVERSE.

I have no any supernatural husband or progeny in the heaven. Rather, i consider that all various godlicy forms are my progeny. After my first birth on the earth, before creating afresh kingdom on the earth i had manufactured to my own small kingdom as my family. In order to it i espoused with a terrestrial man in direction of the supreme god. His name is shree Muknaram janee & he is a school lecturer in political science. I have two child from him : ~ son - shree Dharmveer janee (D.O.B. = 11 april, 2004 AD) & daughter - Twinkle janee (D.O.B. = 04 june, 2006 AD).

I self & shree ancient power jee are two body & one sweetheart. My soul will be entered into the ancient supreme god ' s supernatural form automatically after my death & then will not be any necessity of separate worshipping of my idol / picture. Terrestrial persons should to worship of only six pictures / idols given by me.

5. ONE SYMBOL TWO CHANTS

In order to show homogeneity in my kingdom i gives only one symbol (ॐ) to all my dear earthlings for achieving them godlicy favour to contain on their bodies. I gives two chants : --

1. Shree Gayatri jee chant &

2. Shree Hanumanjee chalisa chant

if the terrestrial people are from any caste, religion, denomination and residency.

OUM

All these three are excess marvellous and in galore supernatural positive energy. All godlicy forms ' domicile of these three. You have to contain " ॐ " symbol and must bath it into godlicy fire flame or smoke and then should to wear it again if " ॐ " is made by gold, silver, iron, bronze, brass, bentex, wood, plastic etc any substance. Due to containing " ॐ " on your body you will gained best sense.

Shree Gayatri jee chant & shree Hanumanjee chalisa chant are the troubleshooter chants. You can invoke its to get done your desired work by the god at worshipping time (morning - evening), at non worshipping time, free time in day or night and in frequency as you like.

Gayatri Mantra

Om Bhur Bhuvah Svah
Tat Savitur Varenyam
Bhargo Devasaya DhiMahi
Dhiyo Yo Nah Prachodayat

Meaning

Oh God, the Protector, the basis of all life, Who is self-existent, Who is free from all pains and Whose contact frees the soul from all troubles, Who pervades the Universe and sustains all, the Creator and Energizer of the whole Universe, the Giver of happiness, Who is worthy of acceptance, the most excellent, Who is Pure and the Purifier of all, let us embrace that very God, so that He may direct our mental faculties in the right direction.

GAAYATRI CHANT

It is not necessary that whenever you bestow the sacrament to the god then you burn to ember and is not necessary that you would bestow at the time of morning - evening. If you are unable to bestow the sacrament duly then you can bestow in any time in the day or night. You can bestow home made sweet condenced milk or home made " HALWA " (of carrot, lentil, semolina, flour etc) without any ember in emergency. If there is not available home made then you can bestow market made in emergency. You should to ring the bell into the gods ' ears necessarily.

6. DISSOLUTIONS OF RITUALISMS

There is an austerity of ritualisms in present human life of universe in every situation and at each site. Here people are muddle headed and become confused in superstitious notion of occultists and priests. They pressurized with economic expenditures of without any reasons. So we determined to efface all old - evil - retualisms and to replace new - easy - rules instead of its : --

1. Stop to all types of sacrifices and offering prayers to god in front of fire if there is a birth, marriage, death or any other occasion because fire and water are life threatening so do not worship to its.

2. Do not revolve to the god in the worship places. In order to establish uniformity in the whole earthlings you have to make only one worship place for one family and should to keep six pictures / statues in it & then start duly worship. Do not hail to worship place on any religion based name but enunciate paradise / heaven to it.

3. Do not put on the god statue - your / your child ' s cutted hairs and nails because its are inferior and expellable substances.

4. Stop to sacrifices - prayers in front of fire and circumambulations in someone ' s marriage. In the first stape - Compare to horoscopic compatibility of

prospective couple by a scholar astrologer. After then - in an auspicious moment, for discharge of peacefully - happy life,, to do pray from the god by anyone member of their family. There have to flame a lamp of ghee in front of home ' s paradise. Put the lamp of ghee in a neat & clean plate and then circulate it in anti clockwise direction with speaking the " AARATI " of the god. After then erect the prospective couple on the stage. In that time, the bride should be right side of the groom. Thereafter, they both should habilitate the rings and wedding garlands to each other. Thereafter, their parents / guardians have to place hand in hand each other of bride and groom. Then their seat have to change, should to separate the hand and should to sit down both the bride & the groom. In it situation the bride should sit down in groom ' s left side as in the picture of the god couple. Thereafter you may do photography - videography etc. Thereafter again erect the couple. Then the groom will be enrobed wedding necklace into the bride ' s neck and will put vermillion on bride ' s middle line of her head. Now, the marriage is done.

5. Do not bury dead body. should not make any dome on grave and should not worship to grave dome rather have to burn the dead body.

6. Shut down various prevalent deities ' & divinities ' worship places which is made saparately & should stop to hosting of fairs on name of them and do not make unnecessary gathering.

7. If you are doing any fast on name of the god then you will get god grace & your health will be best. But do not organise any accumulate on name of fast as : - teez,

chauth, shashthi, ashtami, ekaadashi, anant chaturdashi, poornima, amaavashya, seven days, sun accumulation, gangour accumulation etc. Just stop these convenes completely.

8. You should to read religious books for increasing your knowledge but do not worship to books, rivers, ponds, lakes, mountains, trees (basil, ficus religiosa, banyan harebell, prosopis cineraria, calotropis, aegle marmelos etc) etc.

9. There must be a lemon plant / tree on the left side of outgoing home gate. River the ganga is started from god shree Shivjee ' s hairs according to mythical fiction but there is not like this at now so you should not put your fore - elders ' bone urn in it .

LEMON

According to social customs there are relatives ' intimates in the family after anyone ' s death till 10 - 12 days. In these days have to put meal and water for dead body ' s soul on outgoing gate ' s left side near lemon plant / tree. In these days, dead person ' s soul can see to all and speaks but alive persons can not see and hear to it. After about 10 - 12 days in auspicious moment all present members or any one member or some members have to consecrate it in front of home paradise by flaming lamp of ghee with speaking aarti. Just after that there will be automatically reborned dead soul by grace of shree ancient power jee which habitanted in lemon tree / plant. You have not to worship the lemon tree / plant.

10. Do not feed any meal to saints / priests / brahmans on the name of fore - elders and stop to giving alms to them.

11. Do not appoint any priest / saint as director for god meeting of someone and should not give any alms to it. Priests / saints are not angels of the god from the heaven.

12. Gold, silver, copper, bronze, brass, bentex etc high priced substances are not holy so do not donate its ' vessels to priests / brahmans but you should donate to meal, water, clothes, shoes and ordinary vessels. You should not donate anything to classical priests /saints /brahmans rather must donate to needies and helpless if he / she is classical gainer also.

13. SUTAK (ritual impurity state) : -- There is not any sutak belong to birth or death in any family and at the time of sun or moon eclipse also. There are not prohibited to taking meal - water and god worshipping in it time. Sutak is not erases by cow ' s mud - urine, daab

grass, gangawater, ganga - coast - clay, milk - curd etc. Rather the word " sutak " is imaginary and a part of ritualism. You can take meal - water and can worship to god easily in it time.

14. Stop to celebrating the festival of "Sheetala Saptamee" Because there is not can destroy a "variola (small pox)" virus by worshipping of a cloth wraped stone & by eating cold meal.

15. Someone do not bath in rivers, ponds, lakes etc drinking water sources individually or in groups. Should not organise fairs at its beach to gathering crowd because its are not holy. Someone can not become holy by bathing in its. Someone ' s sins are not dissolve in its ' water. Rather someone ' s sins are dissolve by atonement. So general public should to become neat and clean the drinking water sources.

16. The god don't meet by pilgrimage but yes, you can go there for tourism. Because of natural fury and stampede there can massacre. So people should god worshipping in their own home.

17. " Pathwaree " worshipping which is made arrounded by prosopis cineraria tree at the time of starting journey to river ganga and bestowing of a mature coconut fruit on the border of two villages at the time of marriage procession returning -- are on the name of monsters so stop doing so.

18. Stop to celebrating festivals related to animals ' murder because the god lives in the soul of every vivid creature so the god will be angry by animals ' murder When animals count will be increased then there will be

organic agreeculture by manure. Underground water will be increased, there will be increased vegetations on the earth, will not be effective droudgt - famine - flood and pandemic / epidemic will not be arises. So gentlemen / women should take pure - righteous - veg food rather meat is eaten by woody animals only.

19. We have done void amulet as - auspices - unauspices and evil eye - to glance so now, somebody have not to do misconception as it.

20. All able person serve to the elderly of their family in all honesty but do not celebrate the feast after someone ' s death.

21. Local deities - divinities are great humen so stop to its ' worshipping, bestowing sacraments, stop to ancestors ' feeding and help to their rebirthing by growing lemon plant / tree in your own home necessarily. Then start to worshipping and start to bestowing sacraments to original god forms.

22. In order to loosen in godlicy worshipping rules, i liberate to you from night watching - oblation - unbroken flame and singing hymns on name of the god. The god will not be glad on you so as. Rather they will be glad on you by your true attachment with them.

23. Self urine treatment and cow / ox urine treatment are the so - called madness so do not do like this. Do not drink its and do not bath with its because there is not any benefit of its emitter substances in the human body.

24. I liberate to you all earthlings from commitment to accept " VASTU SHASTRA " ' s rules and tips for your home making and any other building making. All

terrestrial people are free to make any building according to their suitability and your choice at any place and in any time. There will not be any harm to them from its.

25. People are worried without any reason by some concoction rules prevalent in the nature. As : - new bride will not be stayed in her husband ' s home with her mother in law in first " SHRAAWAN " (hindu calendar month) month, cots will not be knited in rain season, married women ' s necklace ' s beads will not be needled in rain season, dirty clothes will not be washed on thursday, stitching of clothes will not be done after seven days of holi festival, milk will not be freezed on " AMAAVASHYA ", curd will not be churned on amaavashya, FAST will be dissolved by eating garlic - onion - edible salt, FAST will be dissolved by coitus, hindus will be breaked " FAST " in day, momdons will be breaked fast in night.............. etc. These all are false pageantry so stop to its. Mean by keeping fast is not related with the sun or the moon but keeping fast is mean by taking one time meal (cereals & lentils) within 24 hours.

7. THE EXPLANATIONS

Many questions are arises into your mind by reading, hearing & knowing my deeds so i gives to you its 'explanations : -

1. Why lamp of ghee ?...... Ghee is made by saturated fatty acids which are of quiet nature. Rather oils are made by unsaturated and turbulent natured fatty acids so both aur brain and life will be quiet and happy by flaming lamp of ghee.

2. Why not an incense stick but why lamp of ghee ?........ You can not see face of the god by flaming an incense stick. Rather your godlicy interview is done by lamp of ghee in which you can see to the god and they can see to you. Then will be your welfare by fall in sight of them on you.

3. Why ring bell at the time of worshipping ?.......... All forms of the god are wake by ringing bell and then they hear your prayer and do your works.

4. Why not bestow coconut fruits to the god ?.......... Coconut is made by oil and is turbulent natured.

5. Why not bestow sweets, hellow sugar - cakes, clout - nails etc ?.......... These are impure, fictitious, adulterated and made by mock milks - oils - ghees.

6. Why bestow home made sweet condenced milk / HALWA ?.......... It is pure, veg and righteous. So the god will do your work purely with honesty after taking its.

7. Why dry cow - mud ?.......... The " Nandijee " ox is divine and active vehicle of god shree " Shivparwatijee ", cow / ox are naive animals, its take veg - righteous meal and its ' mud have a little water - able to make stark.

8. Why put first morsel on cinder ?............. First morsel is of all various vehicles collectively.

9. Why twirl aarti ' s plate and worshipping water anticlockwise ?............ Direction of the supernatural godlicy waves are from north to south (anticlockwise) which is opposite of clockwise screw direction.

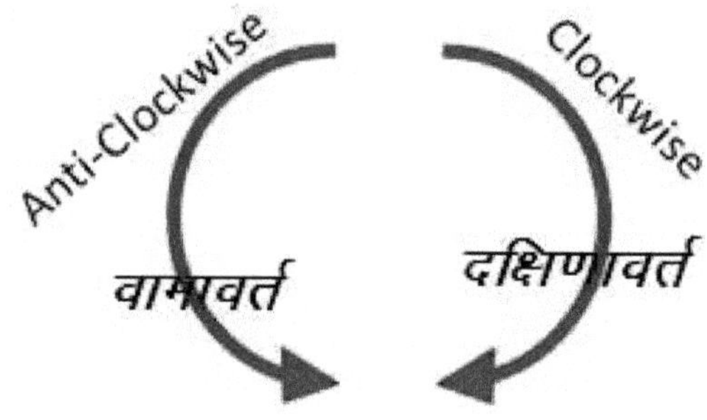

So you will be got godlicy positive - spiritual - supernatural energy by done so. Whereas, we are living on the earth and the earth self rotating in anticlockwise direction so we have to rotate aarati / worshipping plate / water in anticlockwise direction to achieve the physical, mental and spiritual support of this astrological planet.

10. Why pandemic expansions within one hundred years on the earth ?............. Humankinds are alive and closed on the earth standby other astrological planets and effected by it. Relation between the earth and humankinds is as mother and it ' s progenies. Tolerance age of the earth is one hundred years as humankinds '

terrestrial age. So the earth ' s tolerance power concluded for coming one hundred years when earthlings exploit it indiscrimiately and then occurs pandemic on it as signal of holocaust. To postponed it there is necessary for humankinds that they should to exploit limited and balanced of their mother earth. In the form of reimbursement humankinds should to plant planting on the earth and must to increas maximum groundwater level.

11. Why not bestow fruits ?............ Fruits are many types from its ' inner part as some are rotten, sour, bitter, alkaline etc. So someone can not recognize its ' ability from its ' outer surface.

12. Why should be gate of worshipping chamber in north direction ?.................. The earth self is leaned with 23. 5 degree angle towards north pole and we are living on it, maximum population of the world are inhabited on north hemisphere, headquarters of the heaven and the hell are situated on north hemisphere, magnetic force lines in the earth are goes from south to north direction and then eyesight of the god should be on all these processes.

13. Why does maximum miraculous form is god shree Hanumaan jee ' s mountain holder in one hand and mace holder in other hand with flying in air form ?....................In the Raamaayan ' s yuddha kand (Lanka kand) when almighty god shree Raamachandra jee despired and mentally unarmed by his younger brother shree Laxman jee ' s injury and faintness then shree Hanumaan jee saved shree Laxman jee ' s life by bringing the vitalizing herb from hundreds miles far during the

night and unleashed courage to god shree Raamachandra jee. Then they got destroy monsters and their lanka. Where someone worships to god shree Seetaram jee then shree Hanumanjee goes there without any summon and where someone worships to shree Hanumaan jee then shree Hanuman jee goes there with shree Seetaramchandra jee.

14. Why does maximum miraculous and impressive form of the god shree Shivparwati jee - Gajaanand jee riding over the Nandi jee ox ?....................Shree Nandi jee is an active vehicle which destroys harmful viciouses present nearby devotees by driving away from them. So devotees gain extra advantages of shree Nandi jee ' s activeness by worshipping of it formed picture.

15. Why did shree Nostradamus jee wrote that i would be declared " thursday " as my holiday ?................ The god selected him because he was in all conscience of heart and knower of many subjects (astrologer, teacher, doctor, author, soothsayer etc). He did many predictions about me by inspiration of godlicy feelings. But the godlicy feelings are so short timely that someone can not consider its exactly. In this order by fault considering he considered my birth day (thurs day) as my holiday. But I will work continuously within all days and nights for safety of my own kingdom without any holiday.

16. God shree Hanuman jee is a man or a monkey in his authentic form ?.............God shree Hanuman jee is not a monkey of red mouth indeed. He has not any tail. He went to Shree Lanka according to Sundarkand of the Raamaayan after contained with monkey ' s body by his amusement masquerade. In real form, god shree

Hanuman jee is the man of big body whose face is big, rounded and fair (gora = wheatish) colored. So do not paste oil - vermilion (red lead) and red moli - panna on his statue. The green shining mountain is in his one hand on one shoulder and a mace is in another hand on another shoulder. His half pant and stole is red colored.

17. How the supernatural structure of goddess shree earth jee ?................. Yes, with her physical form, shree earth jee have her supernatural / spiritual structure as other female godlicy forms. Her face is globe shaped rounded, big sized and wheatish colored. She wears multi colored sarees. I done interviews with her many times. I gives most respect to her. In the first i greet to her and after then i greet to shree sun jee before my waked up in the morning. You all should to do so. All ten astrological planets effect human body so all earthlings should to worship its. Divine vehicle of the earth jee is " shree air jee " and the sun jee ' s divine vehicle is " shree white horse jee ". Other eight astrological planets has their own souls, supernatural structures and divine vehicles likewise. I does interviews with them according to my situations.

8. MISCELLANEOUS

1. All earthlings are free from my side for translation of my all books in any language at any time and at any place.

2. I instructs to all universal creatures that they should keep distance from hot spots of the heaven and the hell situated on the earth at about 45 degree northern latitude.

3. The supreme god shree ancient power jee makes halffemale god form of all godlicy forms by connecting with their half left part. She gives to them power of the third eye from her right eye. Although i am as it terrestrial form of her yet it work is mine after my birth so my right eye is most powerful and big in size naturaly from left eye since my childhood.

4. There is a vibration in my both hands since my birth because of supernatural anticlockwise waves presence in my body. My doctors most tried to stop these vibrations but they have not success.

5. There is not any device made in whole the universe to measurement of supernatural waves present in my body. Whenever some new research is moves then it is done by godlicy inspiration and order. The science is made by the god self but sometimes the godlicy feelings are transient so researcher can not consider properly and he / she can not reach to proper result. It same happened at the making time of D.C. battery.

6. I purchased online USA made ghostmeter but it was not effected on my supernatural spiritual positive energy waves.

GHOSTMETER

It could not measure my supernatural energy because there is arises clockwise waves from it ' s D. C. battery but godlicy waves direction is anticlockwise. If someone change position of D.C. battery ' s anode and cathode then it ' s current direction can be change. Science is made by godlicy inspiration through human. Science, religion and spiritualism are mutually corelated deeply.

7. I invites suggestions from all terrestrial people to tell me about some evils prevalent in any caste - religion - denomination - country on the earth. So that i will announce to erase it and then will be replace new - easy rules instead of its.

8. In order to bring similarity in whole the universe I invites to artists for making three - D statues of final six pictures finalized by me.

9. You have not to speak different various aarati rather, on the occassion of joy (as birth, marriage, home entrance, deepaawali etc), you should to speak only one aarati given by me in next chapter with flaming lamp of ghee. But yes, you should speak the aarati without flaming any lamp to pleasure of the god in any time of day or night also and more than one time. Importance of the aarati is equal to shree gaayatri jee mantra and shree hanuman jee chalisa.

10. The India is nation of theists and vegetarians so the god got birth in it at every time. The god shree Vishnu jee got birth ten times in it. His tenth Kalki incarnation was shree Ramdev jee in fifteenth century. In apast some years, indians increased intoxications and meat swallowing. With its they started to worshipping of monsters. So offences are increased here. Because of it, " covid - 19 virus " wreaked havoc here in 2021 AD. I adjurated to all indians that they must avoid to all types of intoxications - meat eating and indian must to stop monster worshipping + start to god worshipping.

11. Whenever some forecasting be on the earth then it done by a person through the god self and the god do it true on coming appropriate time.

12. As far as possible fulfilment of daily necessity of lipid have to got by ghee against meat, fish, egg and transfats (vegetable ghee). Because of non veg feeding, the god will be angry and cholesterol will be increased in body. At the time of processing of refining and double refining edible

oils and vegetable ghee, there is such as a method in ferment its at heavy temperature - pressure with mixing many types chemicals in its. Then by leaking of its there are make many toxic substances in its which produce abdominal irritation, acidity, obesity, fatty liver, high BP, heart diseases, brain stroke, gastricity, dryness of skin, pain in bone ' s joints, cholesterol increasing etc problems in human body. Whereas ghee has short chain fatty acids so it is easy to digestion and metabolism. Ghee has vitamin - A - D - E - K, calcium, phosphorus, potassium and other minerals which make strengthen to bone joints, increases eyes lustre, make radiant skin. Ghee has not any cholesterol but someone must to use ghee in limited quantity. Obesity increases by deeply fried foods. Deep fried meal is most harmful, less than fried food and minimum baked for digestive system. So families must to do animal husbandry of dairy cattles and should produce to pure ghee in their own home. If you will be nourished to animals then will become balanced ecosystem and there will not be come any epidemic / pandemic in forthcoming hundred years. You have to satisfy your body ' s fatty acid supply by dry fruits.

13. Occultists mislead to many villagers that blue - violet colour is poison ' s colour so do not use it colour ' s clothes, shoes, bangles, hose, gloves, coat, umbrella etc. But i say to you that it color is the almighty god ' s color and very auspicious color. It is a misconceptions that son will make his new separate home in north side of his old home. But i say that you are free for making your home in any direction and on any place as suitable for you then no any harm will you gained. All members of a family will be go out for coming seven days if a specify bird " gu

- gu " has sat down on their home. Its misconceptions are very highly promps and superstitions so do not do like this. You will not be gained any harm.

14. As far as possible, you have to take fresh home made meal because do not available complete nutrients in readymade potted market (fries, salty, savoury, crispy, pasta, lasagna, maggie, pickles, marmalade, jam, jelly, sauce, biscuits, noodles, cold drinks etc) food. There are mixed up pesticides and many types chemicals in its for not to rotenning and deteriorationing. These pesticides and many types chemicals do not digestionable and excretionable. Rather, these are collect in muscles and organs which become cause of many dangerous diseases in the future. So do not give to take these market readymade potted food to your children to eat & drink and do not take you self also. You should to do the supply of body ' s vitamin - C by fresh sour fruits instead of medicines. You must to take various types germinated cereals and lentils then you will be gained plentiful nutrition.

9. ONE MORE RESEARCH : - SCHIZOPHRENIA

Schizophrenia is the most dangerous mental disorder in all other mental diseases. It is monster generated disease in which patient feels scary shadows appearing or he / she to be confused about someone ' s presence. It disease spreads by worshipping to kaal bhairav monster and it ' s partner seven ladies monsters, by bestowing sacraments to them, by eating their sacraments, by containing their symbols on body, by putting ill sight of occultist on someone etc reasons. From them monsters ' ill shadows be effected on person ' s mind.

Patient started to sunk deeply in it after happening it disease. Patient of schizophrenia be dependent on others because it was unable to care itself. It resisted to it ' s medicinal treatment also. Thus, person used to be prospectless and desperate. Patient felt specific taste and smell without any substance presentation. It be confused by it ' s surrounding people that they were conspiracing opposite to it. Patient kept watching continuously for long time in the empty space and it can not focused it ' s own sight on one thing. Afflicted ' s susceptibilities were die and it was not feel cognitions of happiness and sorrowness. It felt that there was many divine powers in itself. There could complaint of personality disorder in it.

Patient was listen strange voices and it was feel thus atmosphere as was not actually. It was not agree to accept that there was not anything surrounded his / her / it ' s. It thought that surrounding persons were trying prove wrong to him / her forcibly. Actually mind of it was not able to it ' s own thinking but it ' s outer mind (id) was accepted incoming voices and replied. Because of loss of inspiration in patient his / her daily working power was finished as ~ it was not take interest in cooking food and washing clothes etc necessary works also.

Patient was starting to go away from the society and oblivious from it ' s disease. Patient ' s power of scrucing up his / her / it 's future and power of again life starting there were minimized and at last finished. Patient was startle from others and could not talk to them. It ' s inner brain neurotransmitter (dopamine and serotonin) were imbalanced and then it tried to suicide.

Because of evil eye of an occultist i self has undergone by it situation in 2013 when my family members stoped my god worshipping, my father had died and when i knew about my own godlicy truth then i could not believe in my self and i thought that i was only an ordinary lady then how i could be the supreme god and the universe maker ?............. Then i feared and trembled, my self confidence droped, i felt in dipression and started trying to suicide. Then my family members treated me by psychiatrists. At last, supreme god shree ancient power jee made me healthy and strong.

My illness was only an ethereal chance so that i can aware my universal people by my sensations. Public must to stop monsters ' worshipping completely and have start to god worshipping. They should to treatment patients by psychiatrists then it disease will be disappeared.

10. AARATI

Aarati hriday vaasiyon ki, jay - jay dusht naashiyon ki.

Sahaay kare deen - heeniyon ki, jay - jay dusht naashiyon ki..

1. Sarv shree gajaanand jee bole, mata - pita ki jay bole.

Dooje shree aadyashakti jee bhee, apana paraakram tole..

Aarati hriday vaasiyon ki..................................jay - jay dusht naashiyon ki.

2. Ham sajeev praniyon ko, shree brahma jee ne janm diya.

Maata shree saraswati jee ne ham sabko guru gyan diya..

Aarti hriday vaasiyon ki..................................jay - jay dusht naashiyon ki.

3. Bolo to shree vishnu jee hai, hamaare sabake paalanahaar.

Aur shree maata laxmi jee hai, hamaari aishvarya ki daataar..

Aarati hriday vaasiyon ki..................................jay - jay dusht naashiyon ki.

4. Kaho to sankatmochak hai, shree seetaramchandra jee ka darabaar.

Aur shree hanuman jee to hai, hamaare apane sipahasaalaar..

Aarati hriday vaasiyon ki..................................jay - jay dusht nashiyon ki.

5. Shree shivparvati jee dekhe hamen, baithe door himaalay se.

Hamen poorn aayu dena, rakhana door narakaalay se..

Aarati hriday vaasiyon ki..................................jay - jay dusht naashiyon ki.

6. Ham sabaki hai vinati, aab dekho unse aaj.

Ham ye chahen shree das grah jee, rakhe hamaari laaj..

Aarati hriday vaasiyon ki..................................jay - jay dusht naashiyon ki..

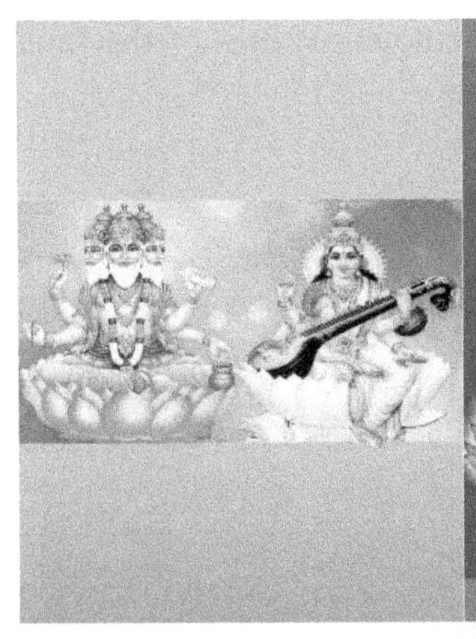

These are final six very miraculous pictures of the total god forms.., mentioned below : -

Contact

Shree Shiv Shakti Offset And Printing

Ads: Opposite Panchayt Samiti Baytu Distt. Barmer (Raj)

Mob. 9799629758

भाग - २

1. एलियनों की कार्य पद्धति

इस भौतिक संसार से परे भी एक और संसार है जिसे हम आध्यात्मिक दुनिया कहते हैं । उसमें पवित्र दिव्य आत्माएँ निवास करती हैं । उन सबकी निर्माता और निर्देशक श्री आद्यशक्ति जी है जिनके निर्देशन में कार्यानुसार विभिन्न ईश्वरीय स्वरूप, उनके वाहन, एलियन और उड़न तश्तरियां होते हैं और ये सब सजीव होते हैं । दस ज्योतिषीय ग्रह और उनके वाहन भी सजीव होते हैं । सजीवों का शरीर जिन पंचमहाभूतों (पृथ्वी, आकाश, जल, अग्नि और वायु) से मिलकर बना होता है उनमें से केवल पृथ्वी और वायु ही सजीव हैं । अंतरिक्ष माध्यम है । वायु प्राण है - प्राण आत्मा है और आत्मा ही जीवन है । ये सब सगुण और साकार होते हैं लेकिन इन्हें देखने हेतु व्यक्ति के पास तीसरी आँख का होना आवश्यक है जिसे प्राप्त करने हेतु भक्ति और कर्म की जरुरत होती है। भक्ति का मतलब बिना किसी कर्मकाण्ड के विधिवत पूजा से है और कर्म का मतलब उचित समयानुसार कर्तव्य पालन तथा नैतिकता से जरूरतमंदों और असहाय प्राणियों की सेवा और दान - पुण्य करना है ।

एलियनों के वाहन उड़न तश्तरियां होते हैं और वे तीनों लोकों (स्वर्ग, नरक और पृथ्वी / मृत्यु लोक) और संपूर्ण ब्रह्मांड में भ्रमणशील ईश्वरीय रोबोट होते हैं । ईश्वर की ही तरह एलियनों का भी कोई भौतिक शरीर नहीं होता बल्कि वे सृष्टि की श्रमिक दिव्य आत्माएँ होती हैं जो कि विभिन्न ईश्वरीय स्वरूपों के लिए निरन्तर कार्यरत रहती हैं । वे ईश्वर के देवदूत / यमदूत होते हैं । किसी व्यक्ति की पार्थिव आयु पूर्ण होने के बाद उसकी मृत्यु के समय आत्मा को उसके भौतिक शरीर में से निकाल कर एलियन (यमदूत) ही ले जाते हैं जो मृतक को काली छाया के रूप में दिखाई देते हैं । अब प्रकृति में कोई भी देवता या देवियाँ विद्यमान नहीं हैं क्योंकि उन सबका पुनर्जन्म हो चुका है चाहे वे किसी भी जाति, धर्म या संप्रदाय से संबंधित रहे थे । राक्षसों को अनन्तकाल के लिए नरक में डाल दिया गया है । सभी ईश्वरीय स्वरूप (श्री गजानंद जी - आद्यशक्ति जी - शिवपार्वतीजी - ब्रह्मासरस्वतीजी - लक्ष्मीविष्णुजी

- सीतारामचन्द्र जी - हनुमान जी - दस ग्रह जी), उनके वाहन, एलियन और उडऩ तश्तरियां भूख, प्यास, मौसम या जलवायु से अप्रभावित होते हैं ।

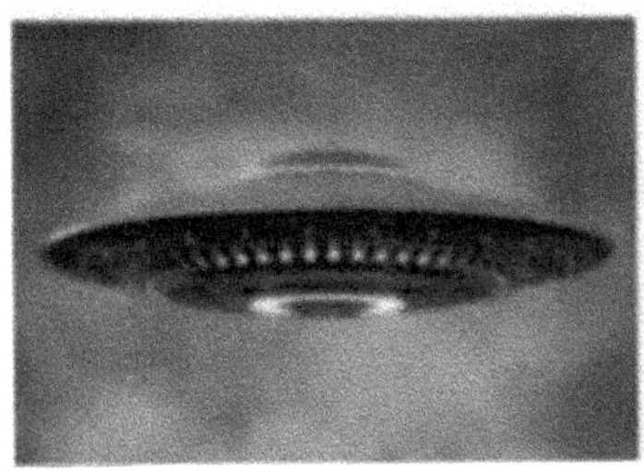

एलियन और उडऩ तश्तरी

एलियन ईश्वरीय रोबोट होते हैं जो स्वयं आपस में एक - दूसरे से, उडऩ तश्तरियों से, विभिन्न ईश्वरीय स्वरूपों से और उनके वाहनों से समान आवृत्ति की मस्तिष्कीय तरंगो से इंटरनेट कनेक्शन के द्वारा जुडे़ रहते हैं और आपस में एक - दूसरे की समान जानकारी से वाकिफ होते हैं । एलियन मानवाकार होते हैं जिसमें दो हाथ, दो पैर और शरीर में सबसे ऊपर मस्तिष्क स्थित होता है क्योंकि इसी स्वरूप में सर्वाधिक बुद्धि और ऊर्जा समाहित होती है । इसीलिए तो सजीवों का क्रमिक विकास मनुष्य के बाद रुक गया । संपूर्ण सृष्टि के समस्त कार्य ईश्वरीय स्वरूपों की देखरेख में एलियनों के द्वारा ही किए जाते हैं । ये प्रतिपल प्रत्येक प्राणी के मन - मस्तिष्क से जुडे़ रहते हैं, उसके मनोभावों तथा कर्मों को देखते, पढते और ऑनलाइन लिखते (क्योंकि स्वर्ग में किसी भी प्रकार का भौतिक दस्तावेज नहीं है) रहते हैं ताकि मृत्युपरांत उसे स्वर्ग या नरक में डाल सके तथा उसके पुनर्जन्म का फैसला उसके पूर्वजन्म के कर्मानुसार कर सके । एलियनों और उडऩ तश्तरियों की ऊर्जा अनन्त, सकारात्मक और ऊर्ध्वगामी होती है । इनके सर्वव्यापी होने की वजह से ही तो ईश्वर सर्वव्यापी हैं ।

एलियन मशीनी मानव होते हैं । मेरी जब भी उनसे मुलाकात हुई तब हर बार मैंनें उन्हें एक वर्दीधारी सिपाही के रूप में देखा जैसे - कभी खाकी वर्दीधारी पुलिस तो कभी सफेद वर्दीधारी सैनिक और कभी

रोबोट के रूप में देखा । एक दिन जब मैं अपने सपने में उनसे मिली तब वे सफेद वर्दी धारण किए हुए मरु मैदान में दूर - दूर खडे हुए थे । तब मेरे दिमाग में विचार आया कि मेरी परीक्षा बहुत नजदीक है जबकि मैं अब तक कुछ भी पढ नहीं पाई तब उन्होंने मुझसे बिना बात किए मेरा विचार समझ कर उसी जगह खडे - खडे बिना कंम्प्यूटर - प्रिंटर - फोटोकाॅपीयर के ही मुझे अपने परीक्षा संबंधी सैलेबस के नोट्स थमा दिए । इस प्रकार से उनकी आयु, कार्यक्षमता और ब्रेनपाॅवर अनन्त है । ईश्वर की प्रेरणा से ही मनुष्य ने एलियन की नकल पर आधारित रोबोट (मशीनी मानव) बनाया ।

2. ना◌ॅस्त्रैदमस की भविष्यवाणी ।।

एशिया का एक विद्वान और महान " शायरन " सभी राष्ट्रों में शान्ति दूत विजेता के रूप में सम्मान पाएगा । इस दौरान एक " एलस (ALUS) " नामक खूनी बर्बर व्यक्ति और उससे प्रभावित दो लोग उसे भयभीत करेंगे लेकिन अंततः उसका हाथ खूनी एलस तक पहुँच जाएगा और वह समुद्री रास्ते से भागने में भी नाकाम रहेगा । दो नदियों के बीच सेना उसे घेर लेगी । उसके किए की सजा क्रुद्ध काला उसे देगा ।

पूरब का वह नेता वायुमार्ग से अपना देश छोड़कर आएगा । वह वायु, जल और बर्फ से ऊपर जाकर अपने दंड का प्रहार करेगा । वह इटली के पहाड़ों और फ्रांस को देखेगा ।

क्रुद्ध काले और सफेद तथा उन दोनों के बीच लाल और पीले अपने - अपने अधिकारों के लिए भिड़ेंगे ।

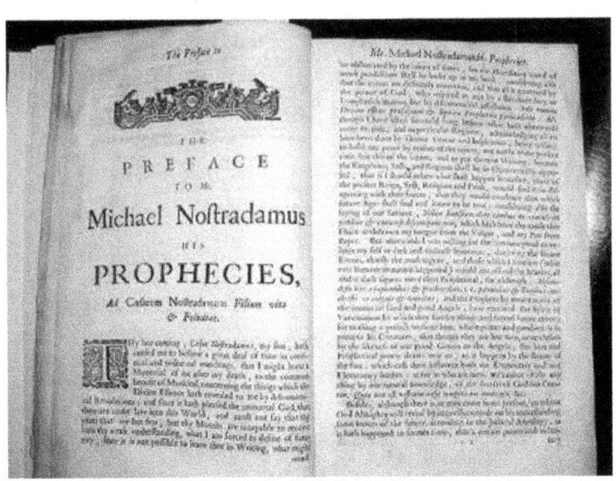
THE
PREFACE
TO M.
Michael Nostradamus
HIS
PROPHECIES,

श्री ना॑स्त्रेदमस जी प्रोफेसीज

स्पष्टीकरण : --

1. यहाँ " मेरे लिए " शायरन " शब्द प्रयुक्त हुआ है । मेरा जन्म नक्षत्रानुसार नाम CH (Chooniya) से आरंभ होता है और यह Cheyren है ।

श्री सुनीता माचरा शक्ति

2. खूनी एलस (ALUS) का मतलब " काल भैरव " राक्षस और उसकी सात सदस्यीय महिला टीम से है ।

3. राक्षस से प्रभावित दो लोगों का मतलब मेरे बडे भाईसाहब और युवा भतीज से है जो किसी दुष्ट तांत्रिक के द्वारा उनकी राक्षसी ब्रेनवाॅशिंग करने के बाद उन्माद रोग से ग्रस्त होकर शराब के नशे की हालत में घर - परिवार के नियंत्रण से बेकाबू आए दिन सड्क दुर्घटना के शिकार हो जाते थे लेकिन मैंनें अपनी ईश्वरीय साधना और दान - पुण्य से उन्हें जीवित और सुरक्षित बचाए रखा और अंततः एक से बढकर एक -- तीन क्रुद्ध काले जी की कृपा से वे अब उन्माद से पूर्णतया मुक्त हैं और सुखी - स्वस्थ जीवन जी रहे हैं ।

4. यहाँ समुद्र का मतलब मेरे अति विशाल हृदय से है जिसमें संपूर्ण सृष्टि के समस्त ईश्वरीय स्वरूप और उनके वाहन समाहित हैं । ये सब हृदय के दाँएँ अर्धभाग और बाएँ अर्ध भाग के मध्य की भित्ति में स्थित तंत्रिकीय गति नियंत्रक (pacemaker) में एक साथ रहते हैं ।

5. चूँकि अब हथियारों से नहीं बल्कि जैविक युद्ध का समय चल रहा है इसलिए यहाँ दो नदियों का मतलब मेरे हृदय के दाहिने अशुद्ध रक्त के हिस्से और बाँएँ शुद्ध रक्त के हिस्से से है जिनके बीच पेसमेकर उपस्थित है ।

6. यहाँ " एलस " को घेरने वाली सेना का अर्थ विभिन्न ईश्वरीय स्वरूपों और उनके वाहनों से है जिन्होंनें उन राक्षसों को घेर लिया ।

7. मेरे पास तीन क्रुद्ध काले जी हैं ---- श्री शनि ग्रह जी की सवारी हाथी जी, स्वयं श्री शनिजी और श्री किंग कोबरा जी । इन तीनों ने मिलकर राक्षसों को नरक में डाल दिया ।

8. इटली के पहाड्रों और फ्रांस को देखते हुए मैं वायुमार्ग से अमेरिका और यूरोप में वहाँ के विभिन्न पुरस्कार लेने जाऊँगी ।

9. यहाँ पर सफेद रंग खूनी राक्षस " एलस " का है जिसने अपने अस्तित्व को बचाए रखने हेतु बहुत संघर्ष किया था लेकिन क्रुद्ध कालों ने उसे अस्तित्व विहीन कर दिया ।

10. लाल - पीले का मतलब यहाँ तांत्रिकों से है जो अब तक जनता की ब्रेनवाॅशिंग करके उनसे धन ऐंठते थे । वे धन के बदले वशीकरण, जादू - टोना, टोटका, अलगाववाद और आतंकवाद फैलाते थे । मुझे अफसोस है कि मेरे देश के प्रधानमंत्री जी से एक तांत्रिक ने भगवान श्री रामचंद्र जी दरबार के पूजागृह का भूमिपूजन करवाते समय ऊपर

वर्णित राक्षस की भी पूजा करवाई थी । मैं यह घटना टेलीविज़न पर देख रही थी । चूँकि उस समय मेरा प्रकटीकरण नहीं हुआ था इसीलिए मैं अ◌ॉब्जेक्शन नहीं कर पाई और मैंनें चुपचाप उस राक्षस को वहाँ से बेदखल कर दिया ।

11. आम जनता से मेरी विनम्र अपील है कि बिना किसी तोड़फोड़ के अहिंसात्मक तरीके से शांतिपूर्वक राक्षसों के पूजा स्थलों से उनकी तस्वीरें /मूर्तियें हटाकर उनके स्थान पर विभिन्न ईश्वरीय स्वरूपों की छ : तस्वीरें / मूर्तियें लगा दो और उनकी विधिवत पूजा करो ।

3. श्री ब्रह्मा जी

श्री ब्रह्माजी का पृथ्वी पर अवतरण मेरे पिताजी श्री मुलतान चन्द माचरा के रूप में 04 अक्टूबर, 1949 ईस्वी को एक गरीब ग्रामीण परिवार में श्री तुलछाराम माचरा के घर में ग्राम पंचायत - बायतु भीमजी, तहसील - बायतु, जिला - बाङमेर, राज्य - राजस्थान (भारत) में हुआ था । वे कुल पाँच (तीन भाई और दो बहनें) भाई - बहन थे । वे उनमें सबसे छोटे थे ।

श्री मुलतान चन्द माचरा

उनकी डेढ वर्ष की वय में ही उनकी माताजी श्रीमती मिरगों देवी का देहावसान हो गया । फिर उनके पिताजी और दो बङी बहनों ने उनको पाल पोषकर बङा किया, पढाया - लिखाया । मेरे दादाजी लकङी और पत्थर टाँकने का काम करते थे । पापाजी के सबसे बङे भाई का देहाँत बचपन में ही हो गया । नौ वर्ष की कच्ची उम्र में पापाजी का बाल विवाह श्रीमती भूरी देवी के साथ हुआ लेकिन उनका गौना सत्रह वर्ष की आयु में हुआ जबकि वे बीएसटीसी की ट्रेनिंग कर रहे थे । अठारह वर्ष में वे तृतीय श्रेणी शिक्षक के पद पर पोस्टेड हुए ।

मेरे मम्मीजी - पापाजी

दोनों भुआएँ ससुराल चली गईं । पापाजी की 19 वर्ष की आयु में मेरे बड़े भाई साहब श्री दीपक कुमार माचरा का जन्म 26 दिसंबर, 1968 को हुआ और चंद दिनों के बाद ही एक महीने के अंतराल से मेरे दादाजी और फिर बड़े पापाजी का हैजा नामक बीमारी से देहावसान हो गया । मेरी बड़ी माँ और उनकी दो बेटियों की सार - संभाल भी मेरे मम्मी जी - पापाजी के भरोसे हो गई । दादाजी और ताऊजी ने लोगों से कर्ज में रुपये उधार ले रखे थे । मेरी ताईजी के गिरवी रखे हुए गहने पापाजी ने छुड़वाकर उन्हें वापस लाकर दिए । उनका वेतन एक सौ रुपए था तो वह उस कर्ज राशि का ब्याज हो जाता था । आए दिन अकाल पड़ते थे । फिर जैसे - जैसे वेतन बढ़ता गया वैसे - वैसे वे अपनी बहनों के परिवारों तथा अन्य गरीब परिवारों की भी मदद करते थे । 17 फरवरी 1971 को मेरी दीदी श्रीमती कमला माचरा का जन्म हुआ और 03 अक्टूबर 1974 को मेरा जन्म हुआ ।

हम चारों भाई - बहनें

मैं चार भाई - बहनों में तीसरी संतान हूँ । मेरी सबसे छोटी बहन भगवती माचरा का जन्म 22 अप्रैल, 1977 को हुआ । मेरी मम्मी जी हाउस वाइफ थी जिनको मेरे पापाजी ने 8 वीं तक पढाया । मम्मी गृहकार्य के साथ खेती बाङी और पशुपालन का काम भी करती थी और हम सब भाई - बहन उनका हर काम में सहयोग करते थे । पापाजी अपनी नौकरी के साथ - साथ उच्च शिक्षा भी ग्रहण कर रहे थे । उन्होंने चिकित्सा विज्ञान की पढाई भी की और अपनी नौकरी के साथ ही ग्रामीण लोगों का लागत मूल्य पर इलाज करते थे । मेरी मम्मीजी ने अपने पास उपलब्ध मामूली गहने भी पापाजी की ट्रेनिंग के आवश्यक खर्च हेतु बेच कर उनका सहयोग किया जबकि बाद के दिनों में उन्होंने फिर से मम्मी जी के सारे गहने बनवा दिए । उनके उच्च शिक्षा के कारण नौकरी में प्रमोशन होते गए । वे तृतीय श्रेणी से द्वितीय श्रेणी और फिर प्रथम श्रेणी अध्यापक बन गए । और अंत में वे 31 अक्टूबर 2009 को शिक्षा प्रसार अधिकारी के पद से रिटायर हुए

। उनके पास कुल सात शैक्षणिक डिग्रियाँ और डिप्लोमा सर्टिफ़िकेट थे ---- बीएसटीसी, बी. ए., बी. एड., एम. ए., एम. एड., वैद्य विशारद और आयुर्वेद रत्न ।

वे बहुत ही महान और उच्चस्तरीय विचारों के व्यक्ति थे और वसुधैव कुटुम्बकम के सिद्धांत की तर्ज पर सबकी मदद करते थे । सबसे मिलजुलकर रहते थे । हम सब भाई - बहनों को उन्होंने अच्छी शिक्षा दिलवाई जबकि आज से करीब 50 वर्ष पहले उस समय में लोग अपने बच्चों को विद्यालय कम ही भेजते थे और लड़कियों को तो बिल्कुल नहीं पढाते थे । उन्होंने ताऊजी की बेटियों को भी बड़ा किया, पढाया और उनकी शादियाँ कीं । आज हम सब छः भाई - बहन सरकारी नौकरी कर रहे हैं ।

लेकिन उनका अपने जीवन काल में प्रकटीकरण नहीं हो पाया कि वे ब्रह्माजी का अवतरण है क्योंकि उन्होंने जरा सी भी भक्ति नहीं की थी । वर्ष 2012 में जब वे बहुत बीमार थे तब मैंनें उनको श्री गायत्री मंत्र बोलने हेतु कहा और श्री हनुमान जी चालीसा लैमिनेशन करके दिया और पढने हेतु कहा लेकिन उन्होंने पढने से स्पष्ट मना कर दिया ।

चूँकि सभी पार्थिव जीवों के जन्मदाता श्री ब्रह्माजी ही होते हैं इसलिए श्री आद्यशक्ति जी को पैदा करने हेतु स्वयं ब्रह्माजी को पृथ्वी पर जन्म लेना पड़ा क्योंकि ऐसा निर्णय लेते समय सभी ईश्वरीय स्वरूपों में आपसी समन्वय और समझ की कमी थी क्योंकि आप सभी पृथ्वीवासियों ने एक ही स्वर्ग में रहने वाले समस्त विभिन्न ईश्वरीय स्वरूपों को अलग - अलग जाति, धर्म और संप्रदाय में बँटकर पूजा जिससे वे तितर - बितर हो गए जिसका हर्जाना समस्त पृथ्वीवासियों को इस रूप में उठाना पड़ा कि जब तक ब्रह्माजी 64 वर्षों तक लगातार मृत्यु लोक में रहे तब तक उनकी अनुपस्थिति में स्वर्ग लोक से जन्म लेने वाले प्राणियों की किस्मत का लेखन एलियन सही ढंग से नहीं कर पाए और आज के मनुष्य भ्रष्ट, बलात्कारी, आतंकवादी, अलगाववादी, नक्सलवादी, दगाबाज, नरहंता और आत्महंता जैसे कुलक्षणों से युक्त हो गए ।

अब हम दोनों पिता - पुत्री अपनी भक्ति और कर्म से निरन्तर ऐसी उल्टी लिखित और नवजातों की किस्मतों को उपयुक्त बनाने हेतु प्रयासरत हैं ।

उन्होंने मुझे अच्छी शिक्षा दिलवाकर काबिल बनाया । समाज में अनेक नवाचार स्थापित किए लेकिन पृथ्वी पर फैली बुराइयों को सुधार नहीं पाए क्योंकि वे फुलफ्लैश और सर्वाधिकार सम्पन्न नहीं थे । मुझे उनके देहान्त (06 नवंबर, 2013 ईस्वी) के केवल 20 दिन पहले ही पता चला कि वे श्री ब्रह्माजी थे लेकिन स्वयं उन्हें यह बात अपने जीते जी कभी पता नहीं चली । उनका देहान्त कैंसर से हुआ लेकिन यह तो एक लौकिक बहाना था । असली कारण तो स्वर्ग में पृथ्वी वासियों के किस्मत का लेखा - जोखा सही करने हेतु उनकी वहाँ सख्त ज़रूरत थी ।

हालांकि उनके अंतर्मन के किसी कोने में यह बात बैठी थी । वे मुझसे कहा करते थे कि पृथ्वी पर कोई व्यक्ति श्री ब्रह्माजी की पूजा नहीं करता और उनका पूजागृह नहीं बनाता और यदि कोई बनाता है तो उसमें मूर्ति रखकर विधिवत पूजा प्रारंभ करने से पहले ही पुजारी की मृत्यु हो जाती है क्योंकि वे सबके जन्मदाता हैं और कोई पुत्र अपने पिता को पैदा नहीं कर सकता ।

अब हमने इस परिपाटी को बदल दिया है । श्री ब्रह्माजी की पूजा उनकी धर्मपत्नी श्री सरस्वती जी के साथ जोडी से शुरू कर दी है । ईश्वरीय स्वरूपों की पूजा जोडी से करने पर सृष्टि वासियों के परिवार स्थिर और स्थाई रहकर फलते - फूलते हैं । अब हमने पापाजी की आत्मा को आदि ब्रह्माजी की आत्मा में प्रवेश करवाकर एकल कर दिया है ताकि उनकी अलग से नाम लेकर या तस्वीर / मूर्ति लगाकर पूजा नहीं करनी पडे । ।

4. मैं

विद्या की देवी श्री सरस्वती जी और ऐश्वर्य की देवी श्री लक्ष्मी जी भी मेरे ही स्वरूप हैं जो अजन्मी और स्वयंभू हैं जिन्हें मैंनें अपने योग और माया से बनाया है । अर्थात् मैं श्री इन वन हूँ बल्कि अन्य सभी स्वयंभू (जो अजन्मे हैं और बिना माता - पिता के हैं) ईश्वरीय स्वरूप भी मेरे योग और माया के द्वारा ही निर्मित हैं इसलिए मैं आॅल इन वन हूँ ।

मेरे पास सभी ईश्वरीय स्वरूपों के सर्वाधिकार सुरक्षित हैं । मेरे पास अनन्त कार्य क्षमता और ब्रेनपाॅवर है । इसलिए अगली बार जब कभी भी ईश्वर को पृथ्वी पर अवतरण की जरुरत होगी तब मैं ही यहाँ पर आकर जन्म लुँगी और उसके पहले श्री ब्रह्माजी को यहाँ जन्म नहीं लेना पडेगा । मैं किसी भी आम आदमी के घर में जन्म लुँगी । मेरा स्वर्ग में कोई आध्यात्मिक / अलौकिक पति या सन्तान नहीं है बल्कि सभी विभिन्न ईश्वरीय स्वरूपों को मैं अपनी संतान समझती हूँ ।

मेरी छोटी सी सृष्टि

पहली बार इस पृथ्वी पर जन्म लेने के बाद मुझे यहाँ नए सिरे से सृष्टि की रचना करने से पहले अपनी स्वयं की छोटी सी सृष्टि बसानी पडी और इसी क्रम में मैंनें श्री सुप्रीम ईश्वर जी के निर्देशन में अपनी 25 वर्ष की आयु में एक लौकिक पुरुष से शादी की जिनका नाम श्री मुकना राम जाणी है और वे राजनीति विज्ञान में स्कूल व्याख्याता है । उनसे मेरे दो बच्चे हैं : - - पुत्र - धर्मवीर (जन्म तिथि = 11 अप्रैल, 2004 ईस्वी) और पुत्री - ट्विंकल (जन्म तिथि = 04 जून, 2006 ईस्वी) । स्वयं मैं और श्री आद्यशक्ति जी ' दो जिस्म एक जान ' हैं और मेरी मृत्युपरांत मैं स्वयं ही श्री आदिशक्ति जी के अलौकिक स्वरूप में प्रवेश कर जाऊँगी और मेरी अलग से तस्वीर / मूर्ति लगाकर पूजा करने की आवश्यकता नहीं रहेगी । सृष्टिवासियों को तो केवल छः तस्वीरों / मूर्तियों की ही पूजा करनी होगी ।

5. एक प्रतीक दो मन्त्र

समस्त सृष्टि में एकरूपता लाने के क्रम में मैं अपने समस्त सृष्टि वासियों को ईश्वरीय कृपा दृष्टि प्राप्त करने हेतु अपने शरीर पर धारण करने के लिए केवल एक ही प्रतीक चिन्ह (ॐ) देती हूँ और दो मन्त्र ----

(1) श्री गायत्री जी मन्त्र और

(2) श्री हनुमान जी चालीसा मन्त्र

देती हूँ चाहे वे किसी भी जाति, धर्म, संप्रदाय अथवा निवास स्थान से संबंधित हो ।

ये तीनों अति चमत्कारिक और आध्यात्मिक सकारात्मक ऊर्जा से भरपूर हैं । इनमें सभी ईश्वरीय स्वरूपों का निवास स्थान एक साथ होता है । ॐ को धारण करने से आपकी कुबुद्धि का क्षय होकर आपको सद्बुद्धि मिलेगी ।

आप ॐ प्रतीक चिन्ह को महीने में कम से कम एक बार ईश्वरीय अग्नि ज्योति या धूम्र से नहलाकर फिर से धारण करें चाहे वह सोना, चाँदी, ताँबा, लोहा जैसी धातुओं से अथवा काँसा, पीतल, बैटैक्स आदि मिश्रधातुओं से या लकड़ी, प्लास्टिक आदि

किसी भी पदार्थ से निर्मित हो ।

श्री गायत्री जी मंत्र और श्री हनुमान जी चालीसा संकटमोचक हैं जिन्हें आप ईश्वर जी से अपना उचित मनोवांछित कार्य करवाने हेतु अपनी सुविधा के अनुसार सुबह - शाम पूजा के समय घी का दीपक जलाकर अथवा दिन या रात्रि में किसी भी समय बिना दीपक जलाए अपने खाली समय में चाहे जितनी बार स्मरण कर सकते हैं ।

ॐ भूर्भुवः स्वः
तत्सवितुर्वरेण्यम्।
भर्गो देवस्यः धीमहि
धियो यो नः प्रचोदयात्॥

अर्थ

उस प्राण स्वरूप, दुःखनाशक, सुखस्वरूप, श्रेष्ठ, तेजस्वी, पापनाशक, देवस्वरूप परमात्मा को हम अंतःकरण में धारण करें। वह परमात्मा हमारी बुद्धि को सन्मार्ग में प्रेरित करे। अर्थात् 'सृष्टिकर्ता प्रकाशमान परमात्मा के प्रसिद्ध पवणीय तेज का (हम) ध्यान करते हैं, वे परमात्मा हमारी बुद्धि को (सत् की ओर) प्रेरित करें।

गायत्री मंत्र

आप ईश्वर जी को जब प्रसाद चढाते हैं तब आवश्यक नहीं कि आप सुबह - शाम ही चढाएँ अथवा अंगारा जलाएँ । मैं आपको नियमों में ढील देती हूँ कि यदि आप विधिवत चढाने में असमर्थ हों तो दिन या रात में किसी भी समय बिना अंगारे के ही उनके श्री मुख से घर में बना मावा या घर में बना हलवा (चाहे वह गाजर, सूजी, आटा, दाल या अन्य वस्तु से निर्मित हो) लगा दें । यदि घर का उपलब्ध नहीं हो तो बाजार से खरीद कर चढाएँ और ईश्वर जी के कानों में घंटी जरूर बजाएँ ।

6. कर्मकाण्ड विघटन

वर्तमान सृष्टि में मानव जीवन में प्रत्येक स्थान और हर परिस्थिति में कर्मकाण्ड की अति हो गई है जिससे यहाँ लोग भ्रमित होकर और ताँत्रिकों तथा पण्डितों के चक्कर में पड़कर अन्धविश्वासों से जकड़ गए हैं और बेवजह के आर्थिक बोझ तले दब गए हैं। इसलिए हमने वर्तमान सृष्टि में व्याप्त सभी प्रकार के व्यर्थ कर्मकाण्डों को मिटाकर उनके स्थान पर सरल नए नियम प्रतिस्थापित किए हैं।

1. यज्ञ और हवन को पूर्णतया बन्द करें चाहे जन्म, शादी, मृत्यु या अन्य कोई भी अवसर हो क्योंकि अग्नि और पानी जानलेवा होते हैं इसलिए उनकी पूजा नहीं करें।

2. पूजा गृहों में ईश्वर जी की परिक्रमा नहीं करें। समस्त सृष्टिवासी एकरूपता लाते हुए एक घर परिवार का केवल एक ही पूजास्थल बनाएँ जिसमें और सभी सार्वजनिक पूजागृहों में एक जैसी छः तस्वीरें / मूर्तियें लगाएँ और विधिवत पूजा करें। पूजा कक्ष का किसी धर्म पर आधारित नाम नहीं रखें बल्कि सभी विभिन्न धर्मावलम्बी सृष्टीवासी पूजास्थल को स्वर्ग / हैवन / पैराडाइज कहें।

3. ईश्वर जी को अपने या अपने बच्चों के बाल, नाखून आदि फैंकने योग्य तुच्छ गन्दी वस्तुएँ उतारकर नहीं चढाएँ।

4. शादी के यज्ञ - हवन और फेरे बन्द करें। किसी योग्य ज्योतिषी से भावी वर - वधू की जन्म कुण्डलियों का अष्टकूट गुण मिलान करवाने के बाद उनकी शादी हेतु उचित मुहूर्त देखकर उस मुहूर्त में भावी वर - वधू के शाँतिपूर्ण - सुखी जीवन निर्वहन हेतु प्रार्थना करते हुए उनके परिवार का कोई भी सदस्य अपने घर के पैराडाइज / हैवन / स्वर्ग में उनके नाम का घी का दीपक जलाएँ। और एक साफ सुथरी थाली में दीपक को रखकर उसे वामावर्त दिशा में घुमाते हुए आरती करें उसके बाद भावी वर - वधू को स्टेज पर ले जाकर खड़ा करें जिसमें वधू को वर की दाहिनी (राइट साइड) तरफ रखें। फिर दोनों एक दूसरे को अंगूठी पहनाएँ और वरमाला पहनाएँ। फिर उनके माता - पिता या

अभिभावक उनके हाथ को एक - दूसरे के हाथ में दें और एक - दूसरे का स्थान बदलकर (जिसमें वधू वर की बाँईं तरफ = लैफ्ट साइड में हो) बैठा दें और उनके हाथ छुड़वा दें । उसके बाद परिजनों या रिश्तेदारों के साथ फोटोग्राफी या वीडियोग्राफी वगैरह करनी है तो करें और तब वर - वधू को फिर से खड़ा करें । अब दूल्हा अपनी दुल्हन को मंगलसूत्र पहनाए और उसकी माँग में सिन्दूर भरे । बस, विवाह प्रक्रिया पूर्ण हुई ।

5. मुर्दा लाशों को गाड़कर उन पर समाधि बनाकर समाधियों की पूजा नहीं करें बल्कि डैड बाॅडीज को जला दें ।

6. पूर्व - प्रचलित स्थानीय देवी - देवताओं के नाम से बने अलग - अलग पूजागृहों को बन्द करें और उनके नाम से मेले नहीं लगाएँ । मेलों के नाम से अनावश्यक भीड़ एकत्र नहीं करें ।

7.यदि आप ईश्वर जी के नाम पर कोई व्रत या उपवास रखते हैं तो आपको उनकी कृपा प्राप्ति के साथ ही आपका स्वास्थ्य भी सही रहेगा लेकिन किसी भी व्रत - उपवास का उजमणा कभी नहीं करें जैसे - तीज, चौथ, षष्ठी, अष्टमी, एकादशी, अनन्त चतुर्दशी, पूर्णिमा, अमावश्या, सातों वार,सूर्य महिमा, गणगौर इत्यादि के उजमणे पूर्णतया बन्द कर दें ।

8. आप अपने ज्ञानार्जन हेतु धार्मिक पुस्तकों को पढ तो सकते हैं लेकिन पुस्तकों, नदियों, तालाबों, झीलों, पहाड़ों, वृक्षों (तुलसी, पीपल,बरगद, आक, धतूरा, खेजड़ी, बेलपत्र इत्यादि) आदि की पूजा - अर्चना नहीं करें ।

9. प्रत्येक घर में बाहर निकलने वाले दरवाजे पर बाँईं तरफ निंबु का पेड़ / पौधा आवश्यक रूप से लगा होना चाहिए ।

निंबु

पौराणिक मान्यतानुरूप गंगा नदी ईश्वर जी की जटाओं में से होकर निकलती थी लेकिन अब ऐसा नहीं है इसलिए आप अपने मृतक पूर्वजों के अस्थिकलश उसमें नहीं डालें बल्कि सामाजिक मान्यतानुसार किसी की मृत्युपरांत आगामी 10 - 12 दिनों तक जब तक रिश्ते - नातेदार शोक - संतप्त परिजनों से मिलने आते हैं तब तक मृतक के घर से बाहर निकलने वाले दरवाजे पर बाँईं (लैफ्ट) तरफ दिन में एक बार मृतक का खाना - पानी रखें । इन दिनों में मृतात्मा अपने आस - पास मौजूद सबको देखती और सुनती है, बोलती भी है लेकिन जीवित लोग उसे देख या सुन नहीं पाते हैं । उसके बाद शुभ मुहूर्त्त में घर के पैराडाइज में घी का दीपक जलाकर मृतक को श्रद्धांजलि अर्पित करें । उसके तत्काल बाद निंबु के पौधे में निवासरत सर्वोच्च ईश्वर श्री आदिशक्ति जी की कृपा से मृतक का पुनर्जन्म हो जाएगा और फिर उसके बाद उसका खाना - पानी नहीं रखें । निंबु के पौधे की पूजा या उससे कोई प्रार्थना नहीं करनी है ।

10. पित्रों के नाम से पण्डितों या ब्राह्मणों को श्राद्ध का खाना नहीं खिलाएँ ।

11. ईश्वर प्राप्ति हेतु अथवा अपने दिए गए दान - पुण्य की साक्षी हेतु किसी पण्डित को अपना गुरु नियुक्त नहीं करें और बदले में उसे दान - दक्षिणा नहीं दें क्योंकि पण्डित / ब्राह्मण स्वर्ग से ईश्वर के मान्तया प्राप्त दूत नहीं होते हैं ।

12. सोना - चाँदी - ताँबा जैसे कीमती धातु, काँसा - पीतल - बैन्टैक्स जैसे कीमती मिश्र धातु पवित्र नहीं होते इसलिए इनके बर्तनों का दान नहीं करें बल्कि खाना - पानी - कपडे - जूते - सामान्य बर्तन इत्यादि जरुरतमंद वस्तुओं का दान दें और वह भी पारम्परिक पण्डितों को नहीं देकर जरुरतमन्दों और असहायों को दें ।

13. सूतक : - घर - परिवार में किसी बच्चे का जन्म होने पर, किसी की मृत्यु होने पर अथवा सूर्य या चन्द्र ग्रहण होने पर किसी भी प्रकार का कोई सूतक नहीं लगता है । ऐसे समय में खाना - पीना या ईश्वर पूजा वर्जित नहीं होती है । गाय का मल - मूत्र, डाब घास, गंगाजल, सोना धातु, दूध - दही या गोपीचन्द (गंगा किनारे की मिट्टी) आदि से सूतक नहीं मिटता बल्कि " सूतक " नाम ही मनगढंत और कर्मकांड का हिस्सा है और ऐसा कुछ नहीं होता । ऐसे समय में आप बेफिक्र होकर खाएँ - पीएँ और ईश्वरीय पूजा करें ।

14. शीतला सप्तमी नामक त्यौहार को नहीं मनाएँ । इस तरह से किसी पत्थर पर कपडा डालकर उसकी पूजा करने और ठंडा खाना खाने से " चेचक " रोग के वायरस नहीं मरते ।

15. नदियों, तालाबों, झीलों आदि पेयजल स्त्रोतों में आप अकेले या सामूहिक स्नान नहीं करें । वहाँ मेलों का आयोजन करके बेवजह भीड नहीं करें क्योंकि ये पवित्र नहीं होते । उनमें नहाकर कोई पवित्र नहीं हो जाता अथवा नहाने वाले के पाप नहीं धुलते बल्कि किसी के पाप तो प्रायश्चित करने से धुलते हैं इसलिए आमजन को चाहिए कि पेयजल स्त्रोतों को साफ और स्वच्छ रखे ।

16. तीर्थयात्रा पर जाने से भगवान नहीं मिलते लेकिन हाँ, आप वहाँ पर्यटन हेतु जा सकते हैं । बल्कि वहाँ भगदड मचने से और प्राकृतिक प्रकोपों से नरसँहार हो सकता है इसलिए अपने ही घर में रहकर विधिवत पूजा - अर्चना करें ।

17. जानवर हत्या से जुडे त्यौहार मनाना बन्द करें क्योंकि सभी जानवरों की आत्मा में ईश्वर का निवास होता है इसलिए जानवर हत्या से ईश्वर नाराज होते हैं । सभ्य जनता को शुद्ध - सात्विक - शाकाहारी भोजन करना चाहिए बल्कि माँस तो जँगली जानवर खाते हैं । जानवरों की सँख्या बढने से प्राकृतिक खाद बढेगी और उससे ह्यूमस बनेगी तथा भूतल पर अधिकतम वनस्पतियाँ लगेंगी जिससे मिट्टी का कटाव नहीं होगा और भूमिगत जल स्तर बढेगा तथा अकाल - सूखा - बाढ का असर नहीं होगा । प्राकृतिक खाद से जैविक खेती होगी जिससे लाइलाज बीमारियाँ नहीं फैलेगी और इस सबके परिणामस्वरूप महामारी (एपीडैमिक / पैण्डैमिक) नहीं होगी ।

18. हरिद्वार जाने के समय खेजडी के वृक्ष के चारों तरफ बनाई गई पथवारी की पूजा और बारात वापसी पर दो गाँवों की सीमा रेखा पर चढाया जाने वाला नारियल राक्षसों को अर्पित होते हैं इसलिए कभी भी पथवारी बनाकर उसकी पूजा नहीं करें और ग्राम पंचायतों के बॉर्डर पर नारियल नहीं चढाएँ ।

19. हमने शकुन - अपशकुन और नजर लगना - उतारना जैसे टोटके निरस्त कर दिए हैं इसलिए अब कोई भी इन्सान इस तरह का वहम नहीं करे ।

20. सभी व्यक्ति अपने परिवार के बुजुर्गों की जीते जी बहुत सेवा करें लेकिन उनकी मृत्युपरांत मृत्यु भोज के नाम पर अनावश्यक खर्च नहीं करें ।

21. स्थानीय देवी - देवता और पितृ महापुरुष होते हैं इसलिए इनकी पूजा करना, प्रसाद चढाना और श्राद्ध के नाम पर इनको खाना खिलाना पूर्णतया बन्द करें । अपने घर में अनिवार्य रूप से निंबु का पौधा / पेड लगाकर इनके पुनर्जन्म होने का रास्ता साफ करें और केवल असली ईश्वरीय स्वरूपों की पूजा करके उन्हें प्रसाद चढाएँ ।

22. नियमों में ढील देने के क्रम में, मैं आपको सृष्टि में पूर्व प्रचलित रात्रिकालीन जम्मा - जागरण प्रथा के तहत रातभर जाग कर ईश्वर के नाम पर यज्ञ - हवन करने, भजन गाने और अखण्ड ज्योति रखने की प्रथा से मुक्त करती हूँ । ईश्वर ऐसे दिखावे से नहीं बल्कि सच्ची आसक्ति से प्रसन्न होते हैं ।

23. स्वमूत्र चिकित्सा और गौमूत्र चिकित्सा तथाकथित पागलपन है इसलिए ऐसा नहीं करें। स्वयं के मूत्र अथवा गाय / बैल के मूत्र को नहीं पीएँ और ना ही इससे स्नान करें क्योंकि इन उत्सर्जक पदार्थों से मानव शरीर को कोई फायदा नहीं होता है।

24. मैं आप सभी सृष्टिवासियों को " वास्तु शास्त्र " के नियमों का पालन करने की बाध्यता से मुक्त करती हूँ। आप अपने घर में अथवा अन्य किसी भी प्रकार के भवन निर्माण के समय जहाँ भी आपको उपयुक्त जगह मिले या जहाँ आपकी इच्छा हो वहाँ कभी भी, किसी भी समय पर मकान के विभिन्न हिस्से बनवाएँ, उससे आपका कभी कोई नुकसान नहीं होगा।

25. कुछ बातों और मनगढंत नियमों से लोग बेवजह परेशान रहते हैं। जैसे शादी के बाद नई दुल्हन पहले श्रावण (हिन्दी कैलैण्डर महीना) के महीने में अपनी सास के साथ ससुराल में नहीं रहेगी, वर्षा ऋतु में चारपाई का नहीं बुनना, वर्षा ऋतु में सुहागिन के गले का नैकलैस के मनके नहीं पिरोना, गुरुवार को मैले कपडे नहीं धोना, अमावश्या को दूध नहीं जमाना, अमावश्या को बिलोना करके दही नहीं मथना, होली त्यौहार के सात दिन बाद तक सिलाई नहीं करना, लहसुन - प्याज - नमक खाने से व्रत का टूटना, रतिक्रिया से व्रत का टूटना, हिन्दुओं का सूर्य को देखकर दिन में व्रत खोलना, मुसलमानों का चाँद को देखकर रात में व्रत खोलना.............इत्यादि। यह सब मिथ्या आडम्बर हैं जिन्हें बन्द कर दें। व्रत रखने का मतलब सूर्य और चन्द्रमा से नहीं बल्कि चौबीस घण्टे में एक बार खाना (अनाज और दालें) खाने से है।

7. स्पष्टीकरण

मेरे द्वारा आपको बताई गई बातों को पढकर, सुनकर या जानकर आपके दिमाग में कई प्रकार के प्रश्न उठ रहे हैं जिनका समाधान मैं यहाँ किए देती हूँ : -

1. " घी " का दीपक ही क्यों ? ---" घी " संतृप्त वसीय अम्लों से मिलकर बना होता है जो कि शान्त प्रकृति के होते हैं जबकि तेल असंतृप्त और अशान्त प्रकृति के वसीय अम्लों से बना होता हैं इसलिए " घी " का दीपक जलाने पर हमारा दिमाग और जीवन शान्त और सुखमय बनता है ।

2. अगरबत्ती क्यों नहीं जबकि दीपक ही क्यों ? ---- अगरबत्ती जलाने से आपको ईश्वर जी का चेहरा नहीं दिखता जबकि दीपक की रौशनी में आपका ईश्वरीय साक्षात्कार होता है जिसमें आप उन्हें और वे आपको देखते हैं । आप पर उनकी कृपा दृष्टि पड़ने से आपका कल्याण होता है ।

3. ईश्वरीय पूजा के समय घंटी क्यों बजाएँ ? ----- घंटी बजाने से सभी ईश्वरीय स्वरूप एक साथ जागृत होकर आपकी प्रार्थना सुनकर आप पर कृपा दृष्टि बरसाते हैं ।

4. ईश्वर जी को नारियल क्यों नहीं चढाएँ ? ----- नारियल तेल से बना होने के कारण अशाँत प्रकृति का होता है ।

5. मिठाईयाँ, बताशे, मखाने आदि क्यों नहीं चढाएँ ? ---- ये नकली दूध, घी, तेल से बने और मिलावटी तथा अशुद्ध होते हैं ।

6. घर में बना मावा / हलवा ही क्यों ? ----- ये शुद्ध और सात्विक होता है इसलिए भगवान जी भी आपके कार्यों को शुद्धता से करेंगे ।

7. गाय / बैल का कण्डा ही क्यों ? ---- बैल ईश्वर श्री शिवपार्वती जी का वाहन है, यह सीधा - शरीफ जानवर है, सात्विक - शाकाहारी खाना खाता है, इनका गोबर सूखा और कण्डा बनने के योग्य होता है ।

8. प्रसाद का पहला कौर अंगारे पर क्यों रखें ? ------ पहला कौर सामूहिक रूप से सभी ईश्वरीय वाहनों का होता है ।

9. पूजा का पानी और आरती की थाली को वामावर्त्त (एंटी - क्लाॅक वाइज) दिशा में ही क्यों घुमाएँ ?

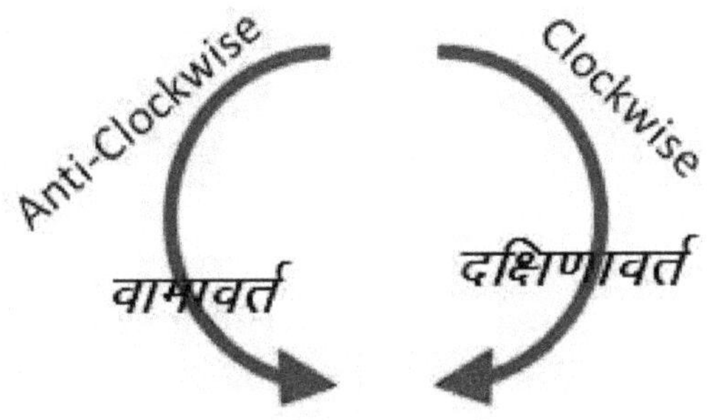

----- ईश्वरीय सकारात्मक आध्यात्मिक ऊर्जा की तरंगों के घूमने की दिशा उत्तर से दक्षिण की ओर (वामावर्त्ती) होती है जो घड़ी की दिशा / दक्षिणावर्त्ती पेच के घूमने की विपरीत दिशा में घूमती है इसलिए ऐसा करने पर आपको ईश्वरीय सकारात्मक आध्यात्मिक ऊर्जा प्राप्ति होगी । चूँकि हम पृथ्वी पर रहते हैं और स्वयं पृथ्वी वामावर्त घूर्णन करती है इसलिए इस खगोलीय ग्रह का शारीरिक, मानसिक और आध्यात्मिक समर्थन प्राप्त करने के लिए हमें भी अपनी पूजा / आरती की थाली / पानी को वामावर्ती घूर्णन करवाना चाहिए ।

10. पृथ्वी पर प्रत्येक सौ वर्षों में महामारी क्यों ?

------ दस ज्योतिषीय ग्रहों में से मनुष्य पृथ्वी के सर्वाधिक नजदीक रहता है और इनसे प्रभावित होता है । पृथ्वी और मनुष्य का माता और सन्तान का सम्बन्ध होता है । जिस प्रकार पृथ्वी वासी सजीव प्राणियों की अपनी उम्र होती है उसी प्रकार पृथ्वी की भी अपनी सहनशक्ति की अवधि सौ साल की होती है । इसलिए जब मनुष्य इसका अन्धाधुन्ध दोहन करते हैं तो आगामी एक सौ वर्षों में पृथ्वी की सहन शक्ति जवाब दे जाती है और प्रलय के संकेत के रूप में यहाँ महामारी प्रकट हो जाती है । इसके प्रबंधन हेतु मनुष्य को अपनी धरती माँ का सीमित और सन्तुलित रूप से दोहन करना चाहिए और उसकी प्रतिपूर्ति के

रूप में इन पर अधिकतम वनस्पतियाँ लगानी चाहिए और इसके साथ ही भूमिगत जल स्तर को अधिकतम बढाएँ ।

11. फलों का प्रसाद क्यों नहीं चढाएँ ?............ फल अन्दर से कई प्रकार के होते हैं जैसे - कुछ सडे हुए, खट्टे, कड़वे,खारे, आदि । इसलिए कोई व्यक्ति बाहर से देखकर उनके योग्य होने की पहचान नहीं कर सकता है ।

12. पूजा कक्ष का दरवाजा उत्तर दिशा में ही क्यों ?.............स्वयं पृथ्वी उत्तर दिशा में साढे तेईस डिग्री के कोण पर झुकी हुई है और हम सब पृथ्वी पर रहते हैं, विश्व की अधिकतम आबादी पृथ्वी के उत्तरी गोलार्द्ध पर बसी हुई है, स्वर्ग और नरक के मुख्यालय पृथ्वी के उत्तरी गोलार्द्ध में स्थित हैं, पृथ्वी के अन्दर चुम्बकीय बल रेखाएँ दक्षिण से उत्तर दिशा में चलती हैं । इन सभी कारणों से ईश्वर जी की नजरें उत्तर दिशा में होनी चाहिए ।

13. ईश्वर श्री हनुमान जी का एक हाथ में पर्वतधारी और दूसरे हाथ में गदाधारी स्वरूप की पूजा ही सर्वाधिक चमत्कारी क्यों ?..................रामायण के युद्ध काण्ड (लंका काण्ड) के दौरान सर्वशक्तिमान ईश्वर श्री रामचन्द्र जी के छोटे भाई श्री लक्ष्मण जी के मूर्च्छित हो जाने पर भगवान श्री रामचन्द्र जी जब बहुत ही हताश और निहत्थे हो गए थे और अपनी हिम्मत हार गए थे तब भगवान और श्रीराम जी के भक्त श्री हनुमान जी ने रातों - रात सूर्य निकलने से पहले सैकड़ों मील दूर स्थित हिमालय पर्वत से एक पर्वत का हिस्सा उठाकर संजीवनी बूटी लाकर दी और श्री लक्ष्मण जी की जान बचाकर श्रीराम जी को हिम्मत बंधाई जिससे वे राक्षसों और उनकी लंका को नष्ट कर पाए । जहाँ प्रभु श्री सीतारामचन्द्र जी का नाम लिया जाता है वहाँ श्री हनुमान जी बिना बुलाए जाकर भक्त की सहायता करते हैं और जहाँ श्री हनुमान जी का स्मरण किया जाता है वहाँ वे श्री सीतारामजी को साथ लेकर भक्त की सहायतार्थ जाते हैं ।

14. ईश्वर श्री शिवपार्वती जी - गजानन्द जी का नन्दी जी बैल पर सवार स्वरूप ही सर्वाधिक चमत्कारी और प्रभावशाली क्यों ?..................श्री नन्दी जी सक्रिय वाहन है जो भक्तों के आस - पास मौजूद नुकसानदायक दुष्टों को उनसे दूर भगाकर नष्ट कर देते हैं इसलिए इस

स्वरूप की पूजा करने से भक्तों को श्री नन्दी जी की सक्रियता का अतिरिक्त फायदा मिलता है ।

15. श्री ना॑स्त्रेदमस जी ने मेरे बारे में ऐसा क्यों लिखा कि मैं गुरुवार को अपना अवकाश दिवस रखुंगी ?.................. वे अपने दिल से सच्चे थे और कई विषयों के जानकार (ज्योतिषी, शिक्षक, डा॑क्टर, लेखक, भविष्यवक्ता आदि) थे इसलिए ईश्वर जी ने उनसे कई भविष्यवाणियाँ करवाईं । उन्होंने अपनी ईश्वरीय अनुभूति से प्रेरित होकर जब भविष्यवाणियाँ कीं तब ईश्वरीय अनुभूतियों के क्षणिक (कम समय की) होने के कारण उनकी समझ में यह फर्क रह गया कि मेरे जन्म के वार " गुरुवार " को उन्होंनें मेरे लिए अवकाश दिवस लिख दिया लेकिन मैं अपनी सृष्टि की सुरक्षा के लिए यहाँ कोई अवकाश नहीं रखकर दिन - रात लगातार काम करुंगी ।

16. अपने असली स्वरूप में ईश्वर श्री हनुमान जी बन्दर है या मनुष्य ?................. वास्तव में ईश्वर श्री हनुमान जी लाल मुँह के पूँछधारी बन्दर नहीं होकर मनुष्य है । रामायण के सुन्दर काण्ड में वे अपनी माया से लीला रचकर बन्दर का वेष धारण करके श्री लंका गए थे । अपने असली स्वरूप में वे बडे़ आकार के मनुष्य है जिनका बडे़ आकार का - गोरे (गेहुँआ) रंग का - गोल मटोल चमकदार चेहरा है । इसलिए उनकी मूर्ति पर तेल - लाल सिंदूर या लाल मोली - पन्ना नहीं चिपकाएँ । उनके एक हाथ में एक कंधे पर हरे रंग का चमकदार पहाड़ है और दूसरे हाथ में दूसरे कंधे पर गदा है । उनकी हाफ पैंट और दुपट्टा लाल रंग के हैं ।

17. ईश्वर श्री पृथ्वी जी का आध्यात्मिक स्वरूप कैसा है ?............ जी हाँ, अपने भौतिक स्वरूप के साथ ही श्री पृथ्वी जी का अन्य महिला ईश्वरीय स्वरूपों की तरह अपना सुपरनैचुरल स्वरूप होता है । उनका ग्लोब की तरह गोल, बड़ा और गोरे रंग का चेहरा है और वे विभिन्न रंगों की साड़ियाँ पहनती हैं । मेरी उनसे कई बार मुलाकातें होती हैं । मैं उनकी बहुत इज्जत करती हूँ और सुबह उठकर श्री जमीन जी पर पैर रखने से पहले उन्हें प्रणाम् करती हूँ, फिर श्री सूर्य जी को प्रणाम् करती हूँ और उसके बाद पैर आँगन पर रखती हूँ । आप भी ऐसा ही करें । सभी दस ज्योतिषीय ग्रहों का मानव शरीर पर विभिन्न प्रकार से प्रभाव पड़ता है इसलिए इनकी पूजा करना सुखी जीवन हेतु आवश्यक

है । श्री पृथ्वी जी का दिव्य वाहन " श्री वायु जी " है और श्री सूर्य जी का दिव्य वाहन " श्री सफेद घोड़ा जी " है । इसी तरह अन्य आठ ज्योतिषीय ग्रहों की भी अपनी आत्माएँ, आध्यात्मिक स्वरूप और दिव्य वाहन होते हैं । परिस्थितिनुसार मेरी उनसे मुलाकातें होती रहती हैं ।

8. विविध

1. मेरी सभी पुस्तकों का उनकी अपनी लिखित भाषा से किसी अन्य भाषा में अनुवाद कोई भी व्यक्ति, कभी भी, कहीं भी और किसी भी भाषा में करने हेतु मेरी तरफ से स्वतन्त्र है ।

2. सभी सृष्टिवासी सजीव प्राणियों को मैं निर्देश देती हूँ कि वे पृथ्वी पर करीब 45 डिग्री उत्तरी अक्षांश के इर्द - गिर्द ग्लोब पर आमने - सामने उपस्थित स्वर्ग और नरक के हाॅट - स्पाॅट क्षेत्रों से दूर रहें ।

3. श्री आदिशक्ति जी अपने अधीनस्थ सभी ईश्वरीय स्वरूपों से उनके बाँएँ (लैफ्ट) अर्धभाग में जुडी रहकर उनका अर्धनारीश्वर स्वरूप बनाती है और अपनी दाँईं (राइट) आँख से उनको तीसरी आँख की शक्तियाँ प्रदान करती है । उनका एज इट पार्थिव प्रतिरूप होने के नाते मेरे जन्म के बाद से यह कार्य मेरा है इसलिए बचपन से ही मेरी दाँईं आँख प्राकृतिक रूप से ज्यादा पाॅवरफुल और आकार में बाँईं आँख से बडी है ।

4. बचपन से ही मेरे शरीर में आध्यात्मिक सकारात्मक ऊर्जा की वामावर्त तरंगों की उपस्थिति के कारण मेरे दोनों हाथों में कम्पन्न होते रहे हैं जिन्हें मिटाने की कोशिश में मेरे डाॅक्टरों ने मुझे बहुत दवाइयाँ दीं लेकिन उन्हें कोई सफलता नहीं मिली ।

5. मेरी शारीरिक आध्यात्मिक ऊर्जा को मापने का कोई भी यन्त्र अब तक पृथ्वी पर नहीं बना है । पृथ्वी पर जब भी कोई नई खोज होती है तो वह ईश्वरीय आदेश और प्रेरणा से ही होती है लेकिन उनकी ईश्वरीय अनुभूति क्षणिक होती है इसलिए कभी - कभी खोजकर्त्ता की समझ में कुछ फर्क रह जाता है और ऐसा ही दिष्ट धारा की बैटरी बनाते वक्त हुआ ।

6. घोस्टमीटर (ghostmeter = भूतमापी) : -

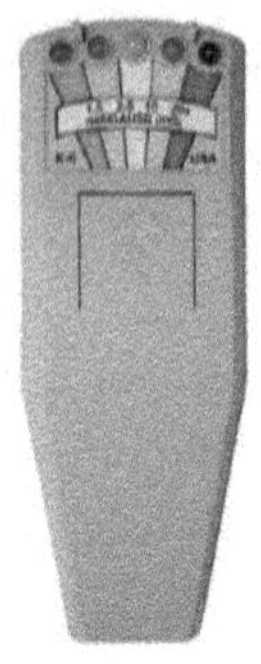

घोस्टमीटर

मैंनें यू. एस. ए. मेड घोस्टमीटर को आॅनलाइन मंगवाया लेकिन वह मेरी आध्यात्मिक सकारात्मक ऊर्जा से प्रभावित नहीं हुआ क्योंकि उसमें लगी डी. सी. बैटरी से दक्षिणावर्त ऊर्जा तरंगें निकलती हैं जो कि ईश्वरीय सकारात्मक आध्यात्मिक वामावर्ती तरंगों से मेल नहीं खातीं। ऐसे यंत्र में लगी डी. सी. बैटरी में लगे कैथोड और एनोड के स्थान बदल देने से उसमें बहने वाली धारा की दिशा बदल कर वह वामावर्ती हो जाएगी। मनुष्यों को प्रेरित करके ईश्वर ने ही विज्ञान को बनाया है। विज्ञान, धर्म और अध्यात्म आपस में एक दूसरे से गहराई से अंतर्संबंधित हैं।

7. मैं समस्त सृष्टिवासियों से सुझाव आमन्त्रित करती हूँ कि पृथ्वी पर कहीं भी, किसी भी जाति, धर्म, सम्प्रदाय या देश में कोई कुरीति अथवा कुप्रथा हो तो आप मुझे उससे अवगत करवाइये जिससे मैं उसे मिटाने की घोषणा कर दुँगी और उसके स्थान पर नए और आसान नियम प्रतिस्थापित कर दुँगी।

8. समस्त सृष्टि में एकरूपता लाने के क्रम में मैं अपने द्वारा अंतिम रूप दी गई छः तस्वीरों से थ्री डी मूर्तियें बनवाने हेतु कलाकारों को आमंत्रित करती हूँ।

9. आपको विभिन्न ईश्वरीय स्वरूपों की अलग - अलग आरती नहीं बोलते हुए खुशी के विशेष मौके पर (जन्म, शादी, गृह प्रवेश, दीपावली आदि) घी का दीपक जलाकर अगले अध्याय में मेरे द्वारा सुझाई गई

केवल एक ही आरती बोलनी है । लेकिन हाँ, आप ईश्वर जी से अपना मनोवाँछित कार्य करवाने हेतु इसे बिना घी का दीपक जलाए ही किसी भी समय एक से अधिक बार अथवा बार - बार भी बोल सकते हैं । इसका महत्व भी श्री गायत्री जी मन्त्र और श्री हनुमान जी चालीसा के बराबर है ।

10. भारत आस्तिकों और शाकाहारियों का देश है इसलिए ईश्वर हर बार यहीं पर जन्म लेते हैं । यहाँ पर श्री विष्णु जी ने दस अवतार लिए थे । उनके दसवें और कल्कि अवतार श्री रामदेव जी पंद्रहवीं शताब्दी में हुए थे । बीते कुछ वर्षों में भारतीयों ने नशा वृत्ति और माँस का सेवन करना बढा दिया और राक्षसों की पूजा करने से अपराध बढ गए इसलिए वर्ष 2021 में यहाँ वायरस जनित बीमारी " कोविड - 19 " ने कहर बरपाया । मेरा सभी पृथ्वीवासियों से अनुरोध है कि आप सभी प्रकार के नशों से और माँसाहार से मुक्त रहें ।

11. पृथ्वी पर जब कभी भी कोई व्यक्ति भविष्यवाणी करता है तब वह स्वयं ईश्वर के द्वारा उसके माध्यम से की जाती है और उचित समय आने पर ईश्वर उसे सच साबित करके दिखाते हैं ।

12. जहाँ तक हो सके वसा की दैनिक आवश्यकता की पूर्ति खाद्य तेलों, माँस, मछली, अण्डा अथवा ट्रांस फैट्स (वनस्पति घी) से नहीं करके दुधारू पशुओं के घी से करें । माँसाहार से ईश्वर नाराज होते हैं और शरीर में काॅलैस्ट्राॅल की मात्रा बढती है । रिफाइंड खाद्य तेलों और ट्रांस फैट्स (वनस्पति घी) की प्रौसैसिंग (रीफाइनिंग और डबल रीफाइनिंग) के समय उनमें कई प्रकार के रसायन मिलाकर अत्यधिक ताप और दाब पर गर्म किया जाता है जिससे उनका क्षरण होता है और जहरीले पदार्थ बनते हैं जो इनका सेवन करने पर मानव शरीर के पेट में जाकर जलन, एसीडिटी, मोटापा, गैस्ट्रीसिटी, ब्रेन स्ट्राॅक, फैटी लिवर, हृदय रोग, उच्च रक्त चाप, त्वचा का रूखापन, जोडों का दर्द और काॅलैस्ट्राॅल वृद्धि जैसी समस्याएँ बढाते हैं । जबकि घी में शाॅर्ट चेन वसीय अम्ल होने के कारण इसका आसानी से पाचन हो जाता है । घी में विटामिन - ए - डी - ई - के, कैल्शियम, फाॅस्फोरस, पोटैशियम और अन्य खनिज लवण पाए जाते हैं जो हड्डियों के जोडों को मजबूत बनाते हैं, नेत्र ज्योति को बढाते हैं, त्वचा को चमकदार और कांतिमय बनाते हैं । घी में काॅलैस्ट्राॅल नहीं पाया जाता है लेकिन

इसका प्रयोग भी सीमित मात्रा में करें । गहरी तली हुई वस्तुएँ शरीर में जाकर सर्वाधिक नुकसान करती हैं उससे कम भुनी हुई और सबसे कम सिकी हुई । इसलिए दुधारू पशुओं को पालें और अपने घर में ही शुद्ध देशी घी का उत्पादन करें । यदि आप अधिकतम पशुपालन करोगे तो उससे पारिस्थितिकी सन्तुलन बनाने में सहयोग मिलेगा और आगामी सौ वर्षों में महामारी जैसी त्रासदी नहीं आएगी । आप आवश्यक वसीय अम्लों की पूर्ति विभिन्न ड्राइफ्रूट्स लेकर करें ।

13. गाँवों के कई लोग तांत्रिकों के बहकावे में आकर नीला - बैंगनी रंग के कपड़े - जूते - जुराब - दस्ताने - कंगन - कोट - छतरी आदि का उपयोग नहीं करते क्योंकि वह जहर का रंग है लेकिन मैं कहती हूँ कि यह स्वयं सर्वशक्तिमान ईश्वर जी का रंग है जो बहुत ही शुभ है । ऐसी मान्यता है कि कोई पुत्र अपने पिता के संयुक्त परिवार से अलग होता है तो अपना नया घर उसके पुराने घर की उत्तर दिशा में ही बनाएगा लेकिन मैं आपको ऐसी बाध्यता से मुक्त करती हूँ कि आपको जहाँ भी, जिस किसी भी दिशा में जगह मिले वहीं आप अपना नया घर बनाएँ । एक विशेष पक्षी " गु - गु " के घर के ऊपर बैठ कर बोल जाने पर लोग आगामी सात दिनों के लिए अपना घर छोड़ देते हैं । सबको विदित रहे कि आगामी समय में आप ऐसा नहीं करें और बेफिक्र रहें कि किसी का कभी कोई नुकसान नहीं होगा ।

14. जहाँ तक हो सके घर का बना ताजा खाना ही खाएँ क्योंकि बाजार में मिलने वाले रेडीमेड और डिब्बाबन्द (चिप्स, नमकीन, कुरकुरे, पास्ता, मैगी, अचार, मुरब्बा, जैम, जैली, साॅस, नूडल्स, बिस्किट्स, कोल्ड ड्रिंक्स आदि) खाने में सम्पूर्ण पोषक तत्व नहीं मिलते हैं और साथ ही उनको सड़ने एवं खराब होने से बचाने के लिए उनमें कीटनाशक और कई प्रकार के रसायन भी मिलाए हुए होते हैं जिनका शरीर में जाकर पाचन और उत्सर्जन नहीं होता है बल्कि वे माँसपेशियों तथा अंगों में जमा होते जाते हैं जो भविष्य में खतरनाक बीमारियों का कारण बनते हैं इसलिए अपने बच्चों को बाजारू - रेडीमेड - डिब्बाबन्द खाना नहीं खिलाएँ - पिलाएँ और आप स्वयं भी ऐसा नहीं खाएँ - पीएँ । शरीर की विटामिन - सी की आपूर्ति दवाइयों से नहीं करने के बजाए ताजा खट्टे फलों से करें । विभिन्न प्रकार के अनाजों और दालों को अंकुरित करके खाएँ जिससे आपको भरपूर पोषण मिलेगा ।

9 एक और रिसर्च : - साइजोफ्रेनिया

साइजोफ्रेनिया अब तक प्रचलित सभी मानसिक रोगों में से सर्वाधिक खतरनाक और राक्षस जनित मनोरोग है जिसमें मरीज को डरावने साए दिखने का आभास या किसी के उपस्थित होने का भ्रम होता था । यह मनोरोग काल भैरव और उसकी साथी सात महिला राक्षसों की पूजा करने, उन्हें प्रसाद चढाकर उसे खाने, उनके प्रतीक चिन्ह शरीर पर धारण करने, किसी दुष्ट तांत्रिक द्वारा कुदृष्टि डालने आदि के कारण दिमाग पर उनके बुरे साए का असर के द्वारा हो जाता था ।

यह बीमारी होने के बाद पीड्ित व्यक्ति इसके दलदल में गहराई से धंसता चला जाता था । साइजोफ्रेनिया का मरीज दूसरों पर निर्भर हो जाता था क्योंकि वह स्वयं अपनी देखभाल नहीं कर पाता और अपने चिकित्सकीय इलाज का विरोध भी करता था । ऐसा इंसान अपनी जिंदगी में नाउम्मीद एवं हताश हो जाता तथा बिना किसी वस्तु की उपस्थिति के ही विशिष्ट गंध या स्वाद का अनुभव करता था । उसे अपने आस - पास उपस्थित लोगों के द्वारा स्वयं के खिलाफ षडयंत्र रचे जाने का भ्रम होता था । मरीज लगातार लंबे समय तक शून्य में देखता रहता और किसी एक चीज या कार्य पर अपना ध्यान केन्द्रित नहीं कर पाता था । उसकी भावनाएँ मर जाती और उसे सुख - दुःख की अनुभूति नहीं होती थी । उसे स्वयं में दैवीय शक्तियाँ होने का एहसास होता था और कभी - कभी उसमें पर्सनैलिटी डिसआॅर्डर की भी शिकायत हो सकती थी ।

पीड्ित व्यक्ति को अजीब सी आवाजें सुनाई देती थीं और ऐसी चीजें या माहौल अनुभव होता था जैसा कि वास्तव में होता नहीं था । मरीज यह मानने हेतु तैयार नहीं होता था कि उसके आस - पास वास्तव में कुछ भी नहीं था । वह यह सोचता था कि लोग उसे जबरन गलत ठहराने की कोशिश करते थे । ऐसी अवस्था में व्यक्ति का वास्तविक दिमाग काम नहीं करता और उसके केवल बाहरी दिमाग (इड) से ही बाहरी आवाजें ग्रहण की जातीं और वही जवाब भी दे देता था ।

मरीज में प्रेरणा की कमी हो जाने के कारण उसकी रोजमर्रा के कार्य करने की क्षमता खत्म हो जाती थी जैसे वह खाना बनाना और कपड़े धोना जैसे आवश्यक कार्यों में भी रूचि नहीं लेता था । पीड़ित व्यक्ति समाज से कटकर और अपनी बीमारी से बेखबर रहता था । मरीज की अपना भविष्य संवार कर फिर से नई जिंदगी शुरु करने की क्षमता कम होते - होते समाप्त हो जाती थी । वह दूसरों से डरने लगता और उनसे बात नहीं कर पाता था । डिप्रेशन से उसके दिमागी कैमिकल - न्यूरोट्रांसमीटर (डोपामाइन और सेरोटोनिन) असंतुलित होकर वह आत्महत्या की कोशिशें करने लगता था ।

एक तांत्रिक की कुदृष्टि के कारण स्वयं मैं भी वर्ष 2013 ईस्वी में इस स्थिति से गुजर चुकी थी । जब मेरे परिजनों ने मेरी ईश्वर भक्ति पर रोक लगा दी थी और उन्हीं दिनों मेरे पिताजी का भी देहावसान हो गया था। और जब मुझे सत्य का ज्ञान हुआ तो मुझे स्वयं पर विश्वास नहीं हुआ कि मैं एक सामान्य महिला होकर कैसे सृष्टि की रचनाकार हो सकती थी । तब मैं डर और वहम से घबरा गई, मेरा आत्मविश्वास बहुत अधिक गिर गया, मैं डिप्रेशन में आकर आत्महत्या की कोशिशें करने लगी थी। तब मेरे परिजनों ने मनोचिकित्सकों से मेरा इलाज करवाया और साथ ही श्री आद्यशक्ति जी ने मुझे पूर्णतया स्वस्थ और तंदुरुस्त बनाया।

मेरा इस रोग से पीड़ित होना सिर्फ एक नैसर्गिक संयोग था ताकि मैं अपनी सृष्टिवासी जनता को अपने अनुभवों के द्वारा जागरुक कर सकूँ।

जन मानस को चाहिए कि वे तत्काल प्रभाव से राक्षसों की पूजा बन्द करके ईश्वर पूजा प्रारम्भ करे ताकि यह रोग समूल नष्ट हो जाए और पीड़ितों का मनोचिकित्सकीय इलाज करवाए ।

10. आरती

आरती हृदय वासियों की, जय - जय दुष्ट नाशियों की ।

सहाय करे दीन - हीनियों की, जय - जय दुष्टनाशियों की ।।

1. सर्व श्री गजानन्द जी बोले, माता - पिता की जय बोले ।

दूजे श्री आद्यशक्ति जी भी, अपना पराक्रम तोले ।।

आरती हृदय वासियों................................ जय - जय दुष्ट नाशियों की ।

2. हम सजीव प्राणियों को, श्री ब्रह्मा जी ने जन्म दिया ।

माता श्री सरस्वती जी ने, हम सबको गुरु ज्ञान दिया ।।

आरती हृदय वासियों................................ जय - जय दुष्टनाशियों की ।

3. बोलो तो श्री विष्णु जी है, हमारे सबके पालनहार ।

और श्री माता लक्ष्मी जी है, हमारी ऐश्वर्य की दातार ।।

आरती हृदय वासियों................................ जय - जय दुष्ट नाशियों की ।

4. कहो तो संकट मोचक है, श्री सीताराम जी का दरबार ।

और श्री हनुमान जी तो है, हमारे अपने सिपहसालार ।।

आरती हृदय वासियों.................................... जय - जय दुष्ट नाशियों की।

5. श्री शिव - पार्वती जी देखे हमें, बैठे दूर हिमालय से ।

हमें पूर्ण आयु देना, रखना दूर नरकालय से ।।

आरती हृदय वासियों...................................... जय - जय दुष्टनाशियों की।

6. हम सबकी है विनती, अब देखो उनसे आज ।

हम ये चाहें

श्री दस ग्रह जी, रखे हमारी लाज ।।

आरती हृदय वासियों.................................... जय - जय दुष्ट नाशियों की।।

अंतिम रूप से सर्वाधिक चमत्कारिक सभी छः ईश्वरीय स्वरूपों की तस्वीरें निम्नलिखित हैं : -

सम्पर्क सूत्र

श्री शिव शक्ति ऑफसेटएण्ड प्रिंटिंग प्रेस

पताः पंचायत समिति के सामने बायतु जिला बाड़मेर (राज.)

मो. 9799629758

भाग - ३

मेरे गाने

1. देशभक्ति का गाना (मेरा भारत देश महान)

मेरा भारत देश महान सबसे प्यारा है

यह है सब रत्नों की खान सबसे न्यारा है ।।

(I) यहाँ सबसे पहले सभ्यता पनपी दिया भाषा का ज्ञान सबसे प्यारा है ।

यह है सब रत्नों की खान सबसे न्यारा है ।।

(II) इसने सबसे पहले ग्रंथ लिखे और वो थे वेद - पुराण सबसे प्यारा है ।

यह है सब रत्नों की खान सबसे न्यारा है ।।

(III) इसने दशमलव की खोज की और ढूँढा शून्य का ज्ञान सबसे प्यारा है ।

यह है सब रत्नों की खान सबसे न्यारा है ।।

(IV) इसने वर्गमूल - घनमूल ढूँढ लिए दुनिया को दिया ज्योतिष का ज्ञान सबसे प्यारा है ।

यह है सब रत्नों की खान सबसे न्यारा है ।।

(V) इसने रामायण - महाभारत लिखे दुनिया को दिया गीता का ज्ञान सबसे प्यारा है ।

यह है सब रत्नों की खान सबसे न्यारा है ।।

(VI) इसने सूर्य - चन्द्र ग्रहण का ज्ञान दिया दुनिया को दिया पंचाँग सबसे प्यारा है ।

यह है सब रत्नों की खान सबसे न्यारा है ।।

2. आध्यात्मिक गाना (मालिक मेरे आओ)

(I) मालिक मेरे आओ हमरी हालत सुधारो ।

गम से त्रस्त जनता को अब शीघ्र दुलारो ।।

चले भी आओ सर्वशक्तिमान, दिल गम से पुकारा हमरी जान भी पुकारे,
गम से त्रस्त जनता को अब शीघ्र दुलारो.....

(II) बीमारी और लाचारी को दूर भगाओ ।

अपने प्यारे बच्चों पर अब पहरा लगाओ ।।

चले भी आओ.....................अब शीघ्र दुलारो ।

(III) बेकारी और मजबूरी को जुदा हमसे कर लो ।

हम हैं आपके बच्चे हमरी पीर को हर लो ।।

चले भी आओ.......................अब

शुघ्र दुलारो ।

(IV) हमने कुदरत को छेड़ा मत उसकी सजा दो ।

फिर से ऐसी गलती ना हो ऐसी दुआ दो ।।

चले भी आओ........................अब शीघ्र दुलारो ।

3. आध्यात्मिक गम का गाना
(आपका प्यार जो हम पाते)

(I) आपका प्यार जो हम पाते तो हम खुशनसीब होते तो हम खुशनसीब होते.........।

कुदरत मेहरबाँ होती तो हम खुशनसीब होते तो हम खुशनसीब होते.............।।

(II) किस्मत में थी जुदाई और कोसों की तनहाई ।

चारों तरफ अँधेरा खुशियाँ ना रास आईं ।।

मेरा हाथ थामे रहते तो हम खुशनसीब होते तो हम

खुशनसीब होते...........।

(III) मझधार में क्यों छोड़ा आपने मुझे रुलाकर ।

खुद आ गए किनारे मेरी कश्ती को डुबाकर ।।

पतवार थामे रहते तो हम खुशनसीब होते तो हम खुशनसीब होते.........।

(IV) दो दिलों में हुई दूरी खुशियाँ रही अधुरी ।

आँखों से अश्क छलके हुई कैसी ये मजबूरी ।।

आप दिल में मेरे रहते तो हम खुशनसीब होते तो हम खुशनसीब होते.........।

(V) आपका प्यार जो हम पाते तो हम खुशनसीब होते तो हम खुशनसीब होते..............।

कुदरत मेहरबाँ होती तो हम खुशनसीब होते तो हम खुशनसीब होते............।

4. गाना (धरती माँ)

धरती माँ का प्यार है, उनका ही दुलार है ।
सच पूछो तो हम पर उनका, सब कुछ ही निसार है ।।
1. यह पालक - पोषक है अपनी, सबकी मददगार है ।
जन्म से लेकर अन्तकाल तक हमरी अपनी यार है ।।
2. इनके नीचे गर्त और, इन पर ऊँचे मीनार हैं ।
हर प्राणी जीवन भर करता, इनका ही दीदार है ।।
3. हम तो करें इनकी पूजा और, इनसे करते प्यार हैं ।
इनके तल पर वृक्ष लगाकर, करते हम शृंगार हैं ।।
धरती माँ का प्यार है, उनका ही दुलार है ।
सच पूछो तो हम पर उनका सब कुछ ही निसार है ।।

5. ईश्वर श्री " सूर्य जी " का गाना

ईश्वर सूर्य चमकते गगन में, दिन भर के गलियारों में ।
रात हुई तब ये ढल जाते ।
क्षैतिज पार अँधियारों में ।।

1. सर्वाधिक एनर्जी दाता, दुनिया के रंगदारों में ।
इनसे सम्पन्न जीवन हमारा, सुखी रहे गुलजारों में ।।

2. भोर हुई तब मुर्गा बोला, बाँग लगाई क्यारों में ।
चिड़िया चहकी कौआ बोला, गूँजा स्वर मीनारों में ।।

3. कोयल की कू - कू सुन दिल है, बाग - बाग मीनारों में ।
सुबह - सवेरे जाग मवेशी, खड़े हुए कतारों में ।।
ईश्वर सूर्य चमकते गगन में, दिन भर के गलियारों में ।
रात हुई तब ये ढल जाते, क्षैतिज पार अँधियारों में ।।

6. मुहब्बत का गाना

मेरा दिल ये कहता है तुम, कुछ और करीब आओ.........
मेरी यादों में समा जाओ...........मेरी यादों में समा जाओ........

1. हर दम करीब थे तुम, जब - जब भी निकट ना थे.........
दिल के करीब लाया, मैंनें तुझे अपना के............

मैंनें तुझे अपनाया, तुम भी मुझे अपनाओ............
मेरी यादों में समा जाओ..........मेरी यादों में समा जाओ....................

2. मुझसे अगर बिछड़ कर, जरा भी तुम दूर जाते........
मर जाते हम कसम से, तुम जो ना पास आते...........

करें बेहद प्रेम तुमसे, जुड़ जाँ से मेरी जाओ.............
मेरी यादों में समा जाओ...........मेरी यादों में समा जाओ.........

मेरा दिल ये कहता है तुम, कुछ और करीब आओ.........
मेरी यादों में समा जाओ..........मेरी यादों में समा जाओ.......

7. आशिकी का गाना

1. तेरी मोरनी के जैसी आँखों का, मैं तो हुआ कायल।
अपनी आँख दिखा तुमने, मुझको किया घायल।।

2. तेरी बाघिन के जैसी चाल का, मैं तो हुआ कायल।
तेज रफ्तार चल तुमने, मुझको किया घायल।।

3. तेरे गुलाबों के जैसे होठों का, मैं तो हुआ कायल।
खुशबू इनकी फैंक तुमने, मुझको किया घायल।।

4. तेरी बाज के जैसी नजरों का, मैं तो हुआ कायल।
चलती नजर फैंक तुमने, मुझको किया घायल।।

5. तेरे चाँद के जैसे चेहरे का, मैं तो हुआ कायल।।
केवल एक झलक देखी, मुझको किया घायल।।

8. सन्तान का गाना

मेरे घर के आँगन में फूल खिले..............
चहकते दो चेहरे मुझे हैं मिले..................

1. बेकरार दिल था बड़ा मालिक मेरे.................

मेरे घर के आँगन में फूल खिले..................
चहकते दो चेहरे मुझे हैं मिले......................

2. बिजली सी चमकी जैसे घर में मेरे.....................

मेरे घर के आँगन में फूल खिले.........................
चहकते दो चेहरे मुझे हैं मिले..........................

3. सुन कर सो जाते हैं ये तराने मेरे.....................

मेरे घर के आँगन में फूल खिले........................
चहकते दो चेहरे मुझे हैं मिले.........................

4. तालीम उनकी अब है भरोसे मेरे..................

मेरे घर के आँगन में फूल खिले........................
चहकते दो चेहरे मुझे हैं मिले........................

5. अरमाँ करेंगे सारे पूरे मेरे...........................

मेरे घर के आँगन में फूल खिले.......................
चहकते दो चेहरे मुझे हैं मिले..........................।।

9. बेवफाई का गाना

मशहूर हो तो क्या हुआ तुम बहुत ही मगरूर हो ।
ऐसी अदा किस काम की तुम बहुत ही मगरूर हो ।।

वादे वफा के करते मगर हकीकत से दूर हो ।
हो शेखियाँ बघारते पर आदत से मजबूर हो ।।

मशहूर हो तो क्या हुआ तुम बहुत ही मगरूर हो ।
ऐसी अदा किस काम की तुम बहुत ही मगरूर हो ।।

लोगों को दिखाते सादगी और अभिमान से चूर हो ।
बाहर से खुश रहते हो मगर पीड़ा से भरपूर हो ।।

मशहूर हो तो क्या हुआ तुम बहुत ही मगरूर हो ।
ऐसी अदा किस काम की तुम बहुत ही मगरूर हो ।।

10. दिल्लगी का गाना

तुम मुझको बुलाते हो ऐसे क्यों सताते हो ।
मैं ये जान ना पाई ऐसे क्यों सताते हो ।।

1. तुम ये आज मत सुनाओ मुझको अपनी दासतां ।
मेरा आज के दिन तुमसे ना है कोई वास्ता ।।

2. तुमने आज क्यों रोका बढकर मेरा रास्ता ।
मेरा आज के दिन तुमसे ना है कोई वास्ता ।।

3. अब तुम कभी मत पूछो मेरा घर और पता ।
मेरा आज के दिन तुमसे ना है कोई वास्ता ।।

तुम मुझको बुलाते हो ऐसे क्यों सताते हो ।
मैं ये जान ना पाई ऐसे क्यों सताते हो ।।

11. गम का गाना

खुशियों का आलम बन गया आँसू का कतरा ।

1. सोचा था मैंनें महकेगा झूमकर मेरा गजरा ।
लेकिन ये जालिम रिश्ता बनकर मेरा गम ठहरा ।।

खुशियों................कतरा ।

2. बडे़ अरमां थे दिल में मगर है आँखों में कुहरा ।
कभी देखने को आतुर थे हरदम तेरा ही चेहरा ।।

खुशियों................कतरा ।

3. चाहते थे हम भी कभी रिमझिम बरसे बदरा ।
अब तो आँसू संग बह गया मेरी आँखों का कजरा ।।

खुशियों................कतरा ।

12. उल्लास का गाना

आज तो हम झूमेंगे और नाचेंगे गाएंगे ।
कोई चाहे हमें रोके - टोके उत्सव मनाएंगे ।।

1. चाँद - सितारों - कलियों - फूलों से तेरी बाॅडी सजाएंगे ।
हद से गुजर कर हम तो तुझे अब अपना बनाएंगे ।।

2. प्यार के राही हम हैं तेरी हम महफिल सजाएंगे ।
सूनी सी तेरी महफिल में हम तो बहारें लाएंगे ।।

3. दिल की तरफ से दो हाथ मिले हैं किस्मत मिलाएंगे ।
मन के साथी दो मीत मिले हैं प्रीत बढाएंगे ।।

आज तो हम...........उत्सव मनाएंगे ।

13." WH " WORD SONG

Where do you live my
यार............................
जहाँ मिल जाए तेरा प्यार..........................
How do you मिले मेरा प्यार........................
जब हो जाए आँखें चार.........................
Who are you मेरे यार.......................
मैं हूँ हमदर्द और तेरा दिलदार..................
What is हमदर्द है यार......................
जो करता है तेरा दीदार....................
When did किया तूने मेरा दीदार.......................
जब तुमसे मिला पहली बार........................
Why did मिले मुझे पहली बार..........................
जब दिल में आया तेरा विचार......................
Which दिल तेरे पास है यार....................
जो तुझे पहनाए बाहों का हार......................
How much तुझे मुझसे है प्यार......................
देख लो यह है अपरम्पार..................
How many your girl friend यार................
सिर्फ तुम ही हो मेरी बहार.........................

14. चाहत का गाना

1. पहली नजर में हमने तुम्हें आजमाया है ।
आँखों में हमने आपका सपना सजाया है ।।

2. बाहों में हमने तुमको कभी झूला झुलाया है ।
गले में हमने फूलों का तुम्हें हार पहनाया है ।।

3. गाना हमने आपका ही गुनगुनाया है ।
कदमों तले ही आपके हमने शीश नवाया है ।।

4. अपनी भी किस्मत का सितारा झिलमिलाया है ।
तुमने हमारे दिल को हमसे ही चुराया है ।।

5. पास हमने तुमको अपने आज बुलाया है ।
एक हसीना से जो हमने दिल लगाया है ।।\

15. जीवन साथी का गाना

1. अपनी चूड़ियों को तुमने जो खनकाया ।
मेरी चाहत को कंट्रोल मैं ना कर पाया ।।

मेरी आशिकी को कोई ना समझ पाया............

2. तेरे पीछे - पीछे मैं तेरे घर आया ।
तेरे डैडी ने मुझे बड़ा धमकाया ।।

मेरी आशिकी को कोई ना समझ पाया..................

3. तेरी राहों में मैं झूमा - नाचा - इठलाया ।
तेरे ब्रदर ने कहर मुझ पर ढाया ।।

मेरी आशिकी को कोई ना समझ पाया..................

4. बात शादी की करने मैं तेरे घर आया ।
तेरे नौकर ने मुझे घर से बाहर भगाया ।।

मेरी आशिकी को कोई ना समझ पाया...............

5. मेरे डैडी को लेकर मैं तेरे घर आया ।
तेरे जैसा जीवन साथी मैंनें तब पाया ।।

मेरी आशिकी को कोई ना समझ पाया................

16. MIX LANGUAGE SONG

Hello my friend तुमने क्या फरमाया............।
How are you friend मैंनें ये फरमाया................।।

1. I am so fine तुमने हर नाज उठाया ।
Oho ! I forgot तुमने मुझे बहकाया ।।

Hello............................ फरमाया ।।

2. Believe to me फिर वही दिल हूँ लाया ।
Star of your destiny मैंनें ही चमकाया ।।

Hello..................................फरमाया ।।

3. After realize you near मैं बहुत इठलाया ।
I am your dutiful तुमने क्यों झुठलाया ।।
Hello............................फरमाया ।।
4. What is the wanting तुमने ही तो सिखाया ।
My heart beats को तुमने ही तो जगाया ।।

Hello..........................फरमाया ।।

17. सावन का गाना

सावन की रिमझिम फुहार सा अपनापन बरसाइए............।
दामिनी की तर्ज पर हमरी किस्मत तो चमकाइए.......।।
1. अपनी बेरुखी भुलाकर हमें तो रिझाइए ।
जानकर अपना हमें पास तो बुलाइए ।।

सावन..............................चमकाइए ।।

2. खुशनसीबी देख अपनी दूर से ना ललचाइए ।
सब कुछ सच जानकर इतना ना घबराइए ।।

सावन..............................चमकाइए ।।

3. होंगे आपके शुक्रगुजार हमसे दूर ना जाइए ।
जरा करीब आकर हमसे हाथ तो मिलाइए ।।
सावन..............................चमकाइए ।।
4. दूर भाग कर आप यूँ हमें ना सताइए ।
आप है हमारे बालम पास तो आइए ।।

सावन................................चमकाइए ।।

18. दुनिया का गाना

हरदम करती मनमानी है ये दुनिया आनी जानी है.........
इस पर देखो तो सागर में ही मौजों की रवानी है...........

1. यहाँ मिट्टी एक तिहाई से कम ज्यादातर तो पानी है ।
लेकिन सब पानी योग्य नहीं ये सारी दुनिया जानी है ।।

हरदम............................. आनी जानी है ।

2. जब हुआ सवेरा पक्षी बोले सुबह गजब ढहानी है ।
यहाँ ऊँच - नीच और भेदभाव तो हर व्यक्ति की जुबानी है ।।

हरदम............................. आनी जानी है ।

3. सूरज ढलते जब क्षैतिज पार यहाँ लगती शाम सुहानी है ।
पक्षी - चौपाए घर जाने की सबने मन में ठानी है ।

हरदम............................. आनी जानी है ।

4. बेटों को पूरी छूट मिले बेटी को कहे सयानी है ।
बेटी भी किसी से कम तो नहीं ये प्रथा ही बहुत पुरानी है ।।

हरदम............................... आनी जानी है ।

5. बेटी को आगे बढने दो उसका चेहरा नूरानी है ।
वह जग में नाम कमाएगी हम सबसे ज्यादा ज्ञानी है ।।

हरदम............................... आनी जानी है ।

19. अपनत्व का गाना

मैंनें सुना था कभी तेरी जुबानी..........।
तुम दरिया हो मेरी और मैं तेरा पानी...........।।

1. ये बातें हो गई अब वर्षों पुरानी ।
मैंनें सोचा था तुम हो मेरी दीवानी ।।

2. मैं भी कभी थी तेरे सपनों की रानी ।
तुमने भी बातें मेरी कई बार मानी ।।

3. लगती थी बातें तेरी जानी पहचानी ।
अब क्यों हुई है मेरी बातें अनजानी ।।

4. पसंद आ गई मुझे अब तेरी जवानी ।
मैं हूँ तेरे दरिया की मौजों की रवानी ।।

मैंनें सुना था...............................तेरा पानी ।।

20. सच्चाई का गाना

जीना है हमको सच की खातिर..................
सच ही लेकिन जीतेगा आखिर................

1. चाहे वो तड़पे चाहे वो तरसे ।
लेकिन है वाकिफ दिल की खबर से ।।

झूठ हो चाहे जितना भी माहिर..................
सच ही लेकिन जीतेगा आखिर.................

2. हारेंगे अंत में एक दिन दुराचारी ।
जीतेंगे आखिर हर बार सदाचारी ।।

हाय रब्बा सच तो बहुत है ताहिर....................
सच ही लेकिन जीतेगा आखिर...................

3. झूठों के पास नहीं है खुदाई ।
बर्दाश्त करनी होगी रब से जुदाई ।।

दुनिया कहती है झूठ है बड़ा ताजिर................
सच ही लेकिन जीतेगा आखिर..............

21. गम का गाना

ढल जा ए गम की रात ए खुशी की सुबह आजा.........
इस बेसुरे आलम में तु अपनी ढपली बजा जा................

1. ये गम की रात देख आकर है बडी कातिल ।
पास मेरे आके बनजा तु मेरी साहिल ।।

ढल जा ए......................ढपली बजा जा........

2. सोचा था मैंनें शाम हुई लेकिन थी बडी जाहिल ।
ए खुशी की सुबह आके बन जा तु मेरी संगदिल ।।

ढल जा ए.....................ढपली बजा जा...........

22. वादों का गाना

तुमने किए थे मुझसे वादे सुहाने...............
अब वो पडेंगे यारा तुमको निभाने................

1. नहीं चलेंगे तेरे कोई बहाने ।
रब्बा आएगा मेरा तुमको झुकाने ।।

2. नाज पडेंगे मेरे तुमको उठाने ।
फर्ज पडेंगे तुमको मेरे चुकाने ।।

3. कच्ची उमरिया तेरी अरे अनजाने ।
लम्बी उमर हो तेरी मेरे दीवाने ।।

4. हम तो लगे हैं अपने रिश्ते उलझाने ।
लग जाएँगे साथी हम इन्हें सुलझाने ।।

तुमने किए....................तुमको निभाने..........

23. सागर किनारे का गाना

हम भी मिले थे कभी सागर किनारे...........।
वो दिन फिर आए मेरा दिल ये पुकारे............।।

1. तुमने रेत पर कई चित्र थे उभारे ।
याद आते हैं फिर वही नजारे ।।

2. बहुत सताते हैं बचपन के गली चौबारे ।
वो दिन फिर आए मेरा दिल ये पुकारे ।।

3. चौबारे से तुमने किए थे कई इशारे ।
याद आते हैं क्या फिर वही नजारे ।।

4. का◌ॅलेज में थे हमने कई साथी सुधारे ।
वो दिन फिर आए मेरा दिल ये पुकारे ।।

5. साथी तेरे हैं अब भी तुझको पुकारे ।
याद आते हैं क्या फिर वही नजारे ।।

हम भी मिले थे कभी सागर किनारे.............।
वो दिन फिर आए मेरा दिल ये पुकारे.............।।

24. JPSB का गाना

जिंस पैंट और सूट बूट पहन मैं काॅलेज जाऊँगा......।
माॅम - डैड को उनके काॅलेज के दिनों की याद दिलाऊँगा.......।।
1. पढने में अच्छी मेहनत कर सबसे अव्वल आऊँगा ।
फ्रेंडशिप के हाथ बढाकर दोस्त भी मैं बनाऊँगा ।।

जिंस पैंट...........................काॅलेज जाऊँगा ।

2. यारों संग पिकनिक मनाकर हसुँगा और हँसाऊँगा ।
एक दूजे संग जो किए वो वादे मैं निभाऊँगा ।

जिंस पैंट...........................काॅलेज जाऊँगा ।

3. यारों संग हमजोली करके पहेलियाँ सुलझाऊँगा ।
एक हसीना को दिल देकर दुल्हन तय कर आऊँगा ।।

जिंस पैंट.........................काॅलेज जाऊँगा ।

4. माॅम - डैड से मशविरा कर आगे बात बढाऊँगा ।
मस्त हसीना को मैं अपनी दुल्हन बना घर लाऊँगा ।।
जिंस - पैंट...........................काॅलेज जाऊँगा ।
मॉम - डैड को उनके काॅलेज के दिनों की याद दिलाऊँगा ।

25. प्रीति का गाना

तेरी गोरी - गोरी बाहों के मैंनें हार पहने - पहने - पहने - पहने.........
ये हार तो बन गए मेरे गहने - गहने - गहने - गहने........

1. मेरे मन मस्तिक में तेरी मूरत है जो समाई ।
सहन ना होगी अब पल भर भी हमसे तेरी जुदाई ।।

तेरी - मेरी जोड़ी जम गई ऐसी क्या कहने - कहने - कहने - कहने..........
तेरी गोरी - गोरी बाहों के मैंनें हार पहने - पहने - पहने - पहने.........
ये हार तो बन गए मेरे गहने - गहने - गहने - गहने...........

2. तेंरे संग आने से पहले हम तो थे हरजाई ।
मेरी उजड़ी सूनी दुनिया तूने आन बसाई ।।

संग मेरे आओ बाबुल का घर छोड़ रहने - रहने - रहने - रहने.........
तेरी गोरी - गोरी बाहों के मैंनें हार पहने - पहने - पहने - पहने.........
ये हार तो बन गए मेरे गहने - गहने - गहने - गहने.......

www.ingramcontent.com/pod-product-compliance
Ingram Content Group UK Ltd.
Pitfield, Milton Keynes, MK11 3LW, UK
UKHW021648190726
13853UKWH00001B/119

9 789354 726095